GREAT
PIKE STORIES

GREAT
PIKE STORIES

FREDERICK BULLER

2009
THE MEDLAR PRESS
ELLESMERE

Published by The Medlar Press Limited,
The Grange, Ellesmere, Shropshire SY12 9DE
www.medlarpress.com

ISBN 978-1-899600-66-3

First published by the Medlar Press as a limited edition 2003
This edition published 2009

Designed and typeset in 11½ on 14pt Bembo Roman.

Produced in England by The Medlar Press Limited,
Ellesmere, England.

Pike Table

One day = thirty six baits.
One bait-can = three men.
Thirty six baits = two runs.
Two runs = one anecdote.
One anecdote = twenty pounds.

H. T. Sheringham

Contents

Introduction

There are many people to thank - mostly writers of long ago who took the trouble to report some extraordinary catch to the sporting press, which for a long period in our history virtually meant *The Fishing Gazette* and *The Field*. I am also grateful to the proprietors of those magazines for employing outstanding editors[1] who had background, vision, imagination and a real empathy with angling authors that fitted them for the task in hand. The editors names - R.B. Marston, R.L. Marston, Francis Francis, H.T. Sheringham and William Senior are almost as well known today as they were to their contemporaries.

I also have to thank individual correspondents, who knowing of my special interest, have taken the trouble to bring items to my attention - like George Higgins did when he wrote to me about stunning pike 'Irish fashion' on ice-covered loughs. How to find anyone to thank for some of the more outrageous stories about pike that have come down to us through the ages is a problem that I shall probably never solve. Having checked references to the finding of the 170lb Lillishall Limeworks pike at Newport that was

1. They were all angling authors themselves.

reported in the Sir John Hawkins edition, 1784, of *The Compleat Angler*, I eventually discovered that his probable source was not an unspecified London newspaper of unknown date as he indicated, but *Aris's Birmingham Gazette* of 21st January, 1767. Sadly that particular issue is missing from the collection at the British Newspaper Library at Colindale. Mention of the British Newspaper Library for the second time brings me to the point where I must acknowledge the huge debt that I owe to the Library. The days that I have spent (mostly Mondays) poring through magazines and newspapers at the BNL at Colindale in north-west London have been among the most rewarding in my life. As an institution I think it is a marvel.

After the demise of *The Fishing Gazette*, the broadsheet *Angling Times* took on the responsibility of reporting big fish, record catches etc. and I thank them for publishing Clifford Warwick's account of his catching of the 'English Record Pike' from the Hampshire Avon. I wish to thank Hugh Mannix, manager of the Bank of Ireland in Enniskillen, who helped me to unravel the mystery of Mrs McManus' pike from Innishkeen - and for sending me a copy of that haunting poem 'The Four Farleys', which for me repeatedly opens the floodgates of memory.

Richard Walker kindly offered to write, especially

for this book, an account of a very large pike that I hooked on Loch Lomond, primarily because he was a witness and saw the pike as it came to the surface within netting range of his boat, but also because he realised that it would be unbecoming for me to write it myself.

Finally, I would like to thank my editors and publishers, that is to say Jon and Rosie Ward-Allen, who approached me to see if I would contribute to such a book (they had the same title in mind), and when I told them that I had a manuscript ready made, they accepted it and published it.

Frederick Buller, June 2003.

Stunning Pike

Frederick Buller

I first became aware of what I thought was the strictly local but unique sport of pike stunning in the early 1960s. In *The Domesday Book of Mammoth Pike* (1979) I wrote:

Before Ireland's Inland Fisheries Trust culled pike on a grand scale, Lough Carra [in County Mayo] was a great pike lake. It was once the scene of a unique sport known as pike-stunning.

Carra is a crystal-clear, shallow lake with a bottom of white marl and when it is very, very cold the bays freeze over with an almost transparent cover of ice.

Whenever this happens, which is infrequently, and as soon as the ice can stand their weight (and sometimes before), a group of dare-devil local lads take to the ice in their search for pike. Once a pike is located, the drill is to surround it while the leader stalks the pike before giving the ice a hammer blow above its head. A well-delivered blow stuns the pike, leaving the dangerous task of retrieving it by means of pulling it through a hole made in the ice. The ring of spotters makes sure that a frightened pike, or a pike escaping from a badly aimed blow, can be relocated.

In 1970 in McEvelly's bar, near Kilavally, Co. Mayo, I met Mr Joseph Donelly of Ballintubber, who was the last man to lead a party of pike-stunners on Carra. Donelly described this unusual sport to me but the spur to record his story came when I found a note of another account of pike-stunning described in J. Wentworth Day's *A History of the Fens* (1595). Wentworth Day acknowledges that John Titterton of Ely wrote the original note in 1898 - but the incident must have taken place before 1850 at which time the mere was drained.

I remember being on Whittlesey Mere when it was frozen tightly over, and the fish were suffocating for want of air. A number of people were following a large pike which swam with its head touching the overhead ice. Evidently it was anxious to get air. One man (Mr Smith, I believe, of Stanground) kept close by, and he at last got someone to go to Mr Bradford, at the Mere's mouth, to borrow an axe: it came, a double-handed one. Smith swung it round his head and brought it down with a mighty crash just over the pike's head. The fish turned over as if shot. A hole was cut, and it was dragged out on to the ice. It was certainly the biggest pike I had ever seen up to that time, but the weight was never known by me. Smith and James Dunthorne were fishermen and gunners, both of Stanground. Dunthorne once almost shot a pike with a big gun.

After my book *Pike* (1971) was published, George Higgins, a regular correspondent of mine from Belfast, who sends me all sorts of helpful notes and references on Irish pike and pike fishing, sent me a piece culled from the October 1956 issue of the now defunct Irish angling magazine *Stream and Field.*

Michael Horan, the author of the article, had preceded me in describing the sport which he called 'Pike Chasing':

Winter's frost quickly lays a glassy sheet of ice on Carra's clear water. On the comparatively shallow water close to the shore the ice reaches a good thickness in a few days. The pike glide shorewards and are clearly visible beneath the ice (Carra, as any angler who has fished it well knows, is exceptionally clear.)

Those taking part in the hunt carefully test the strength of the ice from the shore outwards. This is a very necessary preliminary to the real chase. A crowd of heavily-booted and sturdy men need a strong floor.

Each 'angler' bears a stout stick which he uses for a two-fold purpose, as a balance to steady himself when making a sudden turn at speed, and to smack at his quarry beneath the glassy surface.

The only other piece of equipment necessary is a piece of rag securely fastened over the outer edge of the heel. This enables one to find a grip when a sudden swerve is necessary, as when one is speeding straight ahead full reliance is placed on the toes.

The hunters form a line across the ice till a pike is roused. Then the chase begins. Smack! Smack! Smack! go the heavy sticks above the speeding pike. He swerves, twists and turns, but his pursuers are not to be shaken off. With every second the chase grows. Hob-nailed boots rasp over the ice. A swerve from the elusive pike and the powdered ice rises in a little mist.

The duration of the chase depends on the pike's power of endurance or on the accuracy or luck of his pursuers with a blow of the stick. Occasionally he escapes unscathed. Sometimes the chase ends sharply after a few turns. Often it may go on for an hour before the worn-out fish begins to show signs of exhaustion. The pursuers press their advantage. Turning slowly on his back, the pike yields helplessly. A little hole is pierced in the ice-cover and a flick of a gaff whips him up.

Oftentimes a tap of a stick deftly delivered on the ice above his head leaves the pike stunned and ready for the gaff.

At first sight it may seem a highly dangerous, even suicidal, sport. But to the experienced glider on the ice it has everything that a good healthy sport should have: skill in performance, speed of action, the element of uncertainty, and risk, etc. It requires courage of the true sort. Its devotees would be the very first to decry foolhardiness and recklessness. Nobody has ever got anything more serious than an icy dip while engaged in the chase.

It is an admirable winter sport. A great sport if you are prepared to flash at breakneck speed over a film of ice with a few feet of water beneath. There is no more pleasant way of restoring a glow to cheeks blue with the cold.

Another account of pike-stunning is the one published in *The Field's* Christmas issue of 1890 entitled 'Mallet bait for pike', and attributed only to 'W.S.'

The young squire would be a very clever fellow if other people accepted his own estimation as to his cuteness. It was only the other day, however, that I discovered where he had picked up his notions upon angling. They are curious, not to say old-fashioned. He had been heard at one time to say that, when you have hooked a fish, you should never suffer him to run out with the line; and had also been known to recommend an old Spey salmon fisherman to go about with a long handle to his net, and at the end of it a hook, which ought to be thrust into the fish's mouth as the best way of hauling it out. This, he said, was the most orthodox way of landing a salmon. Being left alone in his father's library one afternoon, I whiled away the time by looking round amongst the old calf-bound treatises that occupied one particular shelf, and I took down a little work, entitled *The Angler's Museum*. As one of its owners had written his name inside the cover, with the date (1787) attached, and as the type and language were old-fashioned, and the paper very faded, I reasonably came to the conclusion that this little treatise - which I have since discovered in *Bibliotheca Piscatoria* [1883] was by Thomas Shirley - was of considerable age, though there was no date upon the title page. In this work I found some absurd rules which had led the young squire astray. One of his habits, which I certainly trust will not grow upon him, I might have traced in Chapter II, which lays down certain cautions 'to be observed by young anglers', and the first of them was this: 'If at any time you happen to be overheated with walking or other exercise, avoid small liquors, especially water, as you would poison; but rather take a glass of rum or brandy, the instantaneous effects whereof in cooling the body and quenching drought are amazing'. It is much to be feared that our young friend has learned to follow this extraordinary advice too literally when walking or other exercise has given him the excuse of considering himself 'over-heated'. But, as has been already hinted, the young squire, though in his way he knew a little of everything as to field sports, was deplorably wrong in some of his notions of angling. I smiled heartily when, after breakfast the other morning, as I was overhauling a pair of skates, he suggested that there was no better bait for pike, when the lake was frozen, than a mallet. It was possible, to be sure, that, in yonder old angling book, trolling with that useful implement had been recommended; but an opportunity for explanation soon came. We both of us went out to practise the outward edge, but the young squire brought with him a thing which he had fetched from the wood-house, and which I believe is called, in some parts of the country, a 'beetle'. At any rate it was a long-handled mallet, which the men use in driving wedges for splitting timber. The young squire affected great mystery when I asked him what he meant by coming out skating with such a ponderous weapon over his shoulder. Did he want to balance himself with it? Did he intend to exercise himself in some amateur job of pile-driving? Was he going to kill a bullock? To all these questions the only reply was a provokingly knowing grin and the words, "You will see presently."

It was beautiful ice that day, for no snow had then fallen, and it was hard and smooth. I noticed that my companion, as we made the irons ring upon the surface, looked keenly about with downcast eyes, as if in search of something. Very soon my eyes also were peering about in the same manner; the ice was strikingly clear, and a beautiful display of weedy growth could be seen through it, as plainly as if the two inches of black ice were but a sheet of plate glass. By-and-by we approached a place where the water shallowed, and then the young squire moderated his pace, and said, "Hold hard, now I will show you what I mean by saying that a mallet is a capital bait for pike." I paused to take a cigar out of my case, and was in the act of lighting it, when I saw him swing the mallet, and bring it down with a thundering thud on the ice, making a magnificent star, with rays extending yards from the central point. Where the heavy head of the implement had struck, I could see underneath the ice a brown form of over two feet long, gradually turning over, so as to exhibit a long streak of white. "He is a 20-pounder at least," cried the young man. By this time I had already discovered that the brown form was that of a pike, which I presume had been effectually stunned by the blow. The young squire, however, was now in a state of great excitement, and, poising the mallet again, he exclaimed, "He is not dead yet, I will give him another." Down came the heavy piece of wood once more in the centre of the star. There was a crash, a loud noise as of an explosion, and there was also a loud splash, for the cute young squire had not reckoned all the chances, and had literally knocked his foothold away. The ice was broken up in a circle, and the breakage luckily ceased about a foot from where I was standing. Being only human, my first instinct was not to rush forward to save the son and heir of my old friend, but to get well out of danger. There was not much danger, however, for the bottom of the lake at that particular part happened to be firmer than it is in some portions with which I am acquainted, and the man of the mallet - literally 'beetle' browed now - was only floundering with the water reaching to about his waist. After he had ejected from his mouth the outlying streams that had got down his throat, I am bound to confess that the instincts of the sportsman at once asserted themselves, and, before he would think of rescuing himself from his (at least) uncomfortable position, he seized the fish across the shoulders, just behind the gills, with the finger and thumb, and threw him, feebly flopping, upon the ice. Then he got to shore, which was not very far off, as best he could, taking the pike with him. This was the only example of mallet bait for pike I have ever seen used. To a certain extent it was successful, and my young friend assured me that he had often, in the days when they could count upon the lake being frozen with some degree of regularity (which he said was when he was a youth in round jackets), killed pike and other fish in that way.

Fly Fishing for Pike

The Field

Of all the accounts that I have read on the subject of fly fishing for pike - one account, in *The Field* of January 18th, 1890, stands out because it is very well written and convinces me that fly fishing for pike in suitable conditions must be the very cream of our sport:

It was getting on in September, the trout fishing in both the lochs, Tummel and Rannoch, was practically over, and friend Tommy and I were not of the fortunate ones who had a grouse moor in the neighbourhood. We had spent the entire summer trout fishing, from the inns of Tummel, Tummel Bridge, and Kinloch Rannoch; but even after such a spell of it, we were loth to leave that lovely country, and return to smoky London town. One evening we were reluctantly discussing this ultimate necessity, when somebody happened to say, "Why don't you have a go at the pike on Loch Chon [Con] before you leave?" Why not, indeed? Anything for an excuse to handle a rod again, and to put off the evil day of departure. Next day was passed muddling about the river below Loch Rannoch, and catching little trout by fair means and foul for bait. Having managed to get some four dozen, we started the following morning at break of day, accompanied by old Rob (a veteran fisherman at Rannoch, and without whom my friend would never stir) and another gillie. I forget what the distance was - some ten miles, I think, across the moors. Anyway, it was sufficiently long to make it desirable that we should not return the same night. We went prepared therefore to sleep out.

Loch Chon is a narrow, rather uninteresting little sheet of water, about a mile long by some two to three hundred yards in width. There were said to be a few trout in it, but to judge from the number of pike, I should think the trout were uncommonly few and far between, and that until they arrived at very substantial dimensions, that they passed a good many sleepless nights. There must have been a good deal of wear and tear in the lives of these fish, speaking generally, I fancy. However, there are trout in the Errochy [Errochty], which flows out of it, and which, after a rapid course through beautiful Glen Errochy, joins the Garry near Struan station. In autumn, too, salmon ascend this pretty little stream for spawning purposes, and much burning of the water used to take place on it. On reaching the loch our first care was to deposit our extraneous belongings at the little broken-down and utterly tenantless bothie by the waterside, where we were to sleep; then after a little well earned refreshment - the tramp had been a stiffish one - friend Tommy and I started in opposite directions along the shore, having ascertained that, without a lot of coopering, the crazy old boat, which lay hauled up near, was quite out of the question. I had been told that the pike were small, but plentiful in Loch Chon; but I was not prepared for the apparently insatiable appetites I found them afflicted with that bright autumn day. It was barely possible to make a cast without a savage rush being made at the bait, and so keen were they that it mattered little if a fish were hooked, played for a while, and fell off; he was bound to come back again, and do his best to be killed. They ran small, did those jack, the great majority weighing from three to five pounds, but they were gifted not only with good digestions, but also with great powers of activity, and they one and all gave capital sport for their size. My stock of natural baits soon came to an end, and I began to wish that instead of my share of the previous day's capture, which amounted to some two dozen only, I had secured ten dozen of [the] little chaps, for I had had a good many torn off the hooks, without any corresponding result in the shape of a fish. Tommy had wisely provided himself with an assortment of ten artificial minnows, all mounted on treble gut; and I could see him on the other side of the loch hard at work hauling out fish. Unfortunately I had neglected this precaution, and found myself possessed of only four rather ragged phantoms. With three of these I managed to secure four more fish of the usual size; then each in turn was incontinently snapped off, and there remained to me only one, attached to a single gut trace - a phantom in very truth. This untempting looking morsel I cast upon the waters with a feeling of absolute certainty that I would see his face again no more; but I was wrong, for at the second throw there was a tremendous swirl, and I inwardly bade farewell to my wretched minnow; but minute after minute passed, and I continued to experience the pleasant sensation of having on something bigger than I had yet hooked that day. Out my friend shot into the lake like a salmon. Every now and again he swept up to the surface, showing the green and glistening flanks of a fine fish, then he would bore about the bottom, as if to get rid of his unpleasant mouthful on the rocks.

With single gut and a stiff rod I could put on no strain, and every second I expected to be the last (as regarded my connection with minnow and pike). At last the latter began to show signs of having had enough, and, after a real good twenty minutes, Donald managed to tail the best fish of the day - a 10-pounder, in fine condition; the single gut had got jammed in between his teeth, hence the result. This, of course, is no very singular occurrence (a friend of mine that same year killed a 30lb pike on Loch Vennachar, when trolling for trout with single gut); but I was considerably pleased with myself at the time. The very next cast a wretched little chap of 3lb or 4lb came at the minnow, and with hardly so much as a pull, walked off with it straight.

My spinning gear was at an end, and so I certainly concluded was my sport; but a thought struck me. A year or two before I had been presented with a marvellous insect, a thing of beauty, a work of art, indeed, which I had been told was a pike fly. I used to contemplate it every now and then with admiration, mingled with awe, and show it as a curiosity. In its wing was no inconsiderable portion of the tail of a peacock, and the wool of various shades, which, along with hackles of gorgeous hue and a foot or two of the very broadest tinsel, formed its body, and would have stuffed a moderate-sized pillow. But the leading features of this remarkable insect were its eyes, formed of two enormous glass beads, and calculated, as I thought, to strike terror into the breast of any fish which caught sight of it; even phlegmatic Donald fetched a longer breath, and took an even larger pinch of snuff when he saw it. As, however, it was the only thing in the shape of bait I had left, I cast it with a mighty effort on the bosom of the waters, on which it arrived with a terrific splash; two seconds had not elapsed before it was grabbed from below the surface, but after a little play the fish fell off. Over him I at once threw the fly again (as I suppose I must call it), and he came at it like a shot, and in due course of time joined his former allies on dry land. My insect proved altogether a great success. Mounted on strong gimp, it defied the best efforts of the Loch Chon pike, and at the end of a good day's sport it retired triumphant, after numerous fights, into his own proper recess in a tin box, with the loss of only one eye. About six o'clock I foregathered with Tommy; he also had had good sport, and killed a lot of fish, but nothing over 5lb, and had lost all his phantoms except two. On reckoning up our joint bag we found that we had killed fifty-two fish, weighing in the aggregate 236lb, a very fair day's work on such a piece of water, as we both thought, and a good share of which had fallen to my much laughed at fly. A more draughty spot than was the bothie in which we spent the night I do not remember; there was no roof to speak of, and the walls were principally composed of large cracks, through which the night wind whistled without intermission. However, we built an enormous fire, and over the toddy Rob and Donald told us some real eye-openers in connection with ghosts, second sight, 'corpse lichts', and so on under the influence of a prolonged dose of which we went off to sleep in our plaids.

The next day we managed to cobble up a few of the holes in the cranky old boat, and, in spite of our sadly reduced stock of gear, I hoped to secure a big one or two. But pike are queer beasts, and, like salmon and trout, they have their humours. We got afloat, and by dint of constant bailing remained so for three or four hours. It was no use. The weather seemed all right; there was a nice little breeze and plenty of clouds in the sky but the fish were off the feed, and, with the exception of half a dozen ordinary sized beasts, we did no good. One grand run I had from certainly the largest sized fish I had seen; he rose at the fly just like a salmon in the middle of the loch, sending the water flying on all sides of him, and the next instant I was fast; he remained on for five minutes, giving capital sport and a lot of excitement.

Indeed, he gave us just a little too much of that, for Donald, whose spell it was then at the pumps, ceased doing his duty for a few seconds to contemplate the performance, and, in consequence, we very nearly went down all standing. Then the big single hook tore away, and we saw Master Jack again no more.

That night we got back to Rannoch pretty well cooked. Two days afterwards we were on our way south, and I have never since experimented with natural minnow or phantom, or gigantic fly, or anything else on Loch Chon.

Postscript:
A pike of 30lb was caught on a fly in Lough Erne in 1870 (*The Fishing Gazette*, 8th March, 1902).

The Hundred Pound Pike

'Mona', The Fishing Gazette *(November 1888)*

'Mona' who lived by Ireland's River Shannon was one of *The Fishing Gazette's* regular correspondents. His name lives on as the inventor of the famous scale for forecasting a pike's weight from its length.

On 24th November, 1888, he wrote a piece which included the following:

Some years ago, at a boarding-school overlooking a certain Irish lake, we used to venture out on the 'bottoms', in March thereabouts, and spear pike coming up from the lake. One afternoon two of us lads, out with the governor's coachman, had killed a few fine fish, throwing the spear, when we suddenly noticed, a few hundred yards off, a few herons on a little island busily engaged in picking the flesh off something. We pulled over, scaring the birds, and there discovered the remains of a pike - the head, naked skeleton, and the tail portion from the vent intact. We stood the remains up on end, and the nose touched mine, though I was five feet ten inches at the time. The head was about the size of a cow's, and the coachman pickled the tail portion, filling a milk 'crock' with it, and that vessel holds from four to six gallons. That pike, in good condition, must have weighed upwards of 100lb. How it met its end is a mystery, for surely those herons could never have killed it. It was probably left high and dry by suddenly falling water.

Yours, &c., Mona.

In the same issue he also recorded the following article, entitled 'The "Arrest" of a Very Big Pike':

Some thirty years ago (about 1850) a pike used to haunt the river Inny, in Longford, whose vast size was the theme of the countryside. Of course, he had been hooked, and with the usual result; not that he could not be killed. 'But if I'd got the tackle to do it,' as a brother of the craft put it, 'he would drown me as sure as there's mate in praties.' In this state of affairs, a member of the Irish constabulary (not then Royal) stationed near, of an ingenious turn, quietly forged, with the assistance of the village blacksmith, a four-foot harpoon, and retiring occasionally to an adjacent and lonely wood, proceeded steadily to practise 'whale-throwing' at a tree. In the course of a month or two his dexterity would have done credit to an assegai instructor in the army of the late lamented Cetewayo. He then procured an empty beer barrel and thirty yards of hemp rope. To attach his harpoon to one end of this rope, and make the other fast to the barrel through the bung, was but a few minutes' work. Then the lid was tightly secured, the whole transferred to his boat, and amid the breathless excitement of the assembled crowd our hardy sub-constable proceeded to reconnoitre. How he manœuvred, how he advanced, retreated, alarmed his quarry, lulled it into careless confidence, stole within two boat lengths of it, the muse shall be silent. But suffice to say, the hissing javelin flew, and, amid the roar of the wildly excited spectators, buried itself deep in the quivering flank of the monster! (Flank is good, but let it pass.) But, mark! In an instant the rope was taut, and the barrel, fouling the seat, was fast, and so under the bridge, like lightning flash, went boat and policeman, with a mighty foaming wake behind them. That evening, as the sun went down, an exhausted policeman was towed ashore with thirty yards of rope, trailing after his boat a dying mighty fish. Spectators held up their hands in awful admiration and wonder as the carcase was pulled out on the bank, and for many a mile the story ran of how the monster of the Inny fell a prey at last to the prowess and cunning of a redoubtable 'peeler'. The fish weighed - well, no matter. Who would narrow a fish of this kind down to a niggardly stone or two? He weighed a few hundredweight's more or less, and peace be to his ashes.

The Lillishall Limeworks Pike

The Marvellous Magazine

In an article entitled 'History of the Pike' in *The Marvellous Magazine* (1822) there was a note culled from a letter published in an earlier London newspaper (2nd January, 1765). The letter, sent from Littleport, was dated 17th December, 1764 and it reported the following incident:

About ten days ago a large pike was caught in the River Ouse, which weighed upwards of 28lb, and was sold to a gentleman in the neighbourhood for a guinea. As the cookmaid was gutting the fish, she found, to her great astonishment, a watch with a black ribbon and two steel seals annexed, in the body of the pike; the gentleman's butler upon opening the watch found the maker's name, Thomas Cransfield, Burnham, Norfolk. Upon a strict inquiry it appears that the said watch was sold to a gentleman's servant, who was unfortunately drowned about six weeks ago, on his way to Cambridge, between this place and South Ferry. The watch is still in the possession of Mr John Roberts, at the Cross Keys, in Littleport, for the inspection of the public.

Later that month, on 25th January, a big pike story that has now become legendary was reported as follows:

On Tuesday last, at Lillishall Limeworks, near Newport, a pool about nine yards deep, which has not been fished for ages, was let off by means of a level brought up to draw the works, when an enormous pike was found. He was drawn out by a rope fastened round his head and gills, amidst hundreds of spectators, in which service a great many men were employed. He weighed 170lb, and is thought to be the largest ever seen. Some time ago the clerk of the parish was trolling in the above pool, when his bait was seized by this furious creature which, by a sudden jerk, pulled him in, and doubtless would have devoured him also, had he not by wonderful agility and dextrous swimming, escaped the dreadful jaws of this voracious animal.

The Voracious Pike

The following tale by 'Zulu' appeared in *The Field* on 10th August, 1901.

Sir, - When trolling for pike in Loch Coultre I hooked on a blue phantom a pike of $7^1/_2$lb. On my gillie taking the fish into the boat, he exclaimed, "This rascal has been hooked before," and sure enough I saw a piece of gimp 18 inches long sticking out of his mouth. We killed the fish, and then, taking hold of the gimp, I hauled on it without effect. Taking a knife, the gillie opened up the fish and cut from its inside a trolling tackle carrying no less than ten hooks, to which was attached as a sinker the hind leg of a toy lead stag about three inches in length. I may say that the tackle bore a very home-made look about it, but the bait was entirely gone, showing it must have been in the fish's stomach for a considerable time.

Can any other angler say with truth that he has killed a pike with a haunch of venison in its stomach?

And some further tales of the voracity of pike. The first is recorded in the *Chelmsford Chronicle*, 1810:

On the 10th inst., as a gentleman of Scarborough and a party of friends were fishing for pike, they hooked and succeeded in securing a pike of the enormous weight of 54lb in which were found four full-grown wild ducks, all of which were, with the pike, dressed for the table.

In the history of Staffordshire it is stated that, at Lord Gower's estate at Trentham, a pike seized the head of a swan as she was feeding under water, and gorged so much as to kill them both. The servants perceiving the swan remain in the same position for a considerable time, went in a boat, and found both swan and pike dead.

Gesner says that a famished pike in the Rhone fixed on the lips of a mule that was drinking, and was drawn out by the beast before it could disengage itself.

A Heart-thumping Experience with a Monster Pike

F.C. Ewald, The Fishing Gazette *(19th February, 1949)*

I was fishing in a very large pond of nearly one hundred acres in extent on an estate in Surrey. Owing to the trees and undergrowth I was unable to use orthodox methods and was casting out my bait underhand, and recovering it the same way.

I had used all my live baits, and just after 2pm I was forced to use a large Silver Devon. The water was gin clear and bank high. After several throw-outs and recoveries I observed a long grey shadow following the bait; which on coming nearer turned out to be a huge pike. His mouth was opening and shutting not 6 inches from the bait, and he followed it right up to the bank until his nose was not more than 1 inch from the toe of my boot. His great eyes looked up at me and he took not the slightest notice of my movements in recovering the line. As I lifted the bait from the water he turned away quite slowly and swam away. My heart nearly stopped beating. Not three weeks before I had landed a 33lb salmon from the River Dee, Aberdeenshire (this fish, by the way, was reported in your paper for the first week in October, 1911), and I could guess the weight of this pike. To return to our pike: with my heart beating like a sledge-hammer I threw out my Devon and recovered it for at least another twenty minutes, and then I saw him following it again. Here was the fish of a lifetime. Would I get him? He did the same thing, snapping at the bait right up to the bank, and when I lifted it clear of the water, to my surprise, he stopped there and looked up at me for fully half a minute, and in desperation I gently lowered the bait right under his nose.

He took it like a flash, and turned away with it. But I was in such a state of excitement by this time that I made a tragic blunder. Instead of striking hard (which I certainly would have done if I had only felt him take it) I paid out line to him, and after carrying the minnow about three yards he let go, and I had missed the chance of a lifetime. This fish weighed over 50lb, of that I am sure; its head was fully 8 inches broad at the eyes, and on measuring the distance which he carried the bait, which I was able to do with almost perfect accuracy, I estimate he measured over 5 feet in length. The butler came down to the lake a little while after and, when I told him what had happened, he said, "Mr. Henderson will be very sorry. This fish has been eating some of the rare wild fowl that visit the lake at this time of the year." He also said the gamekeeper had been told to keep a lookout for it and shoot it on sight. The wife had told me previously that her uncle, when gamekeeper there, had found one dead which weighed 42lb, and only last year one was taken weighing 28lb.

And, believe me, this is the only regret I have in my long experience of fishing - fifty-seven years to be exact. I started with a bent pin at the age of eight. I have had several days' fishing in this same piece of water since those far-off days, but he or she never came my way again. Last year, I observed a perch of fully 4lb making a good meal of a red weed growing by the bank. I have never seen it mentioned in any book that perch feed on weed. I must conclude wishing you and the dear old *Fishing Gazette* the best of luck.

A Lough Conn Pike

'Black Hackle', The Fishing Gazette *(9th December, 1893)*

Sir, - Seeing an article in your issue of 25th ultimo, re. large catch of pike in Lough Sheelin, which I have often trout-fished with success, permit me to relate, for the information of your readers, the capture of the biggest pike I have either heard or read of. It was taken in Lough Conn in the seventies by one of the Royal Irish Constabulary stationed at Crossmolina, a village close by, under the following circumstances:

Like their fellow men, many of the Irish police are bitten with Waltonianism, and Constable Nesbitt strolled out in a leisure hour to woo the fishes. Not with a trolling rod and appropriate gear, however. His soul did not soar beyond a 9-foot pole with some stout cord twisted round a large nail driven transversely through the butt thereof. His tackle consisted in 2 feet of gimp and a huge double hook. Bait he had none, but he hoped to secure a frog, which fortune soon placed in his way. The lough had been recently high and covered a small hollow some 6 feet deep and 30 feet wide near the edge, with which it was connected by a narrow bar about 7 or 8 inches in depth. As the man in green surveyed this wee pool, he suddenly espied a strong swirl in the water, and a back fin of such dimensions as brought Jonah and the whale to his mind. The fish was close and his line was short. With that trust in Providence peculiar to anglers, he deftly swung out his frog a-wooing, and in an instant felt it seized by what seemed a heavy log of wood. Any doubts on this point were speedily dissolved, for the monster made a wild rush, nearly dragging him in, which would probably have made a vacancy in the Force. Feeling that discretion was the better part of valour, he flung in his pole, with which the pike - for pike it was - charged furiously for the bar. It nearly ran aground there, but quickly made a right about turn and disappeared. The pole, however, indicated by its rapid movements that there was not that parting at which we fishers are wont to exclaim "Dear me," or some other mild form of expletive. The constabulary man was a philosopher - most of the gentle craft are - and pulling out a well-coloured clay from his handcuff-case, he coolly lit it, and viewed the proceedings through a soothing cloud of shag. Half an hour passed thus till the rod happened to come within reach, when he seized it, and took a pull. As well pull a shark. He had to let go, and the evolutions continued, the fish showing his fins and tail occasionally as he surged about, and anon a head, which greatly appalled our angler. "Bedad!" quoth he, "tis the divil and no right fish." Another hour passed, Nesbitt now and then getting a pull, till suddenly, with a tremendous rush, the pike ran aground within three yards of his feet. Before it could attempt to dislodge itself Nesbitt threw himself bodily into the water and inserted either hand into the heaving gills of the leviathan. Then ensued a desperate struggle. Pull devil, pull baker, was now the order of the day; but what could a pike, however big, do against a policeman? Bedraggled, panting and gasping, they both at length got high and dry, though the latter word must be taken metaphorically, and the captor, almost as tired as his capture, gazed at it with amazement and triumph. His first thought was, 'Begor! He'll feed the barracks for a week'; his second, 'The dickens a one of the quality ever caught the like.'

He tied it with a piece of his line to the pole, and with the aid of a passing gossoon (Anglice boy) conveyed it proudly to his station, where his comrades became so excited over it, that nothing but a big drink all round could restore their equanimity. Never was worthier fish wetted. It weighed exactly 63lb, and as the Irish police have the Government weights and measures, accuracy on this point cannot be questioned. Two years afterwards, having gone to fish Lough Conn, I visited the post and learned the particulars from the sergeant. He showed me the skull and jaw bones, the latter being fearfully armed and of immense size. They may still be preserved at the Police Barracks. I regret I am unable to give the dimensions of this pike, which has surely beaten the record so far as Irish lough fishing is concerned. - I am, &c.

A Fisherman's Idle Fancies

W. Carter-Platts, The Fishing Gazette *(January 1894)*

I love to sit alone in the firelight in my den, when the lights are turned down and the house is quiet, and think, and think. I do not mean that at such times I worry my brains in those harassing fields of speculation and argument my friend Mr Pritt talks about. Meditation, quite as much as contemplation and argumentation, is a part of the angler's creed, and as I sit and smoke I fling the reins on the neck of idle Fancy, and let her carry me withersoever she may lead. Fancy is a wilful, fickle jade to bestride; but she has a comfortable ambling gait, that suits well the seat of the dreamy angler. It was all through a noisy party of belated roysterers that she pricked up her ears and started off on this canter. The midnight revellers were roaring a chorus at the top of their voices, and as they passed down the road I just caught the lines:

Jack's the king of all,
For they all love Jack!

That set me thinking. It sounded a bit heterodox to me, for I have always been carefully nurtured in the piscatorial faith that the salmon is 'the king of all'. Not being Oscar Wilde, however, I am not infallible, and, perhaps, a Thames fisherman would tell me I was altogether wrong. Let that pass; for 'whosoever king may reign', we are all agreed upon one point, viz, 'we all love jack' - when he is in his proper place, which is at the end of a salmon gut trace, and not on the razzle-dazzle in a trout or grayling stream.

You may regard the pike from a variety of standpoints; look at him through variously tinted glasses. His remarkably healthy appetite - an appetite which is so large, so to speak, that it covers him all over, and there is enough material to spare to mend with - has been the cause of more than one angling writer bestowing civic honours upon him. Cholmondeley-Pennell elevated him to the aldermanic bench long ago, and even years and years before that Fitzgibbon ('Ephemera') likened him to 'the most accomplished corporate officer'. Possibly both authors had in their minds the memory of the alderman who, at the annual civic banquet, invariably commenced operations with a clear space of 8 inches between himself and the table, and then - ate until he touched it! For my own part I cannot, somehow, disassociate him in my mind from the police force. I don't know what first introduced him to my fancy as a 'bobby' - perhaps it was the fact that he is such a bully, or, perhaps, because he is so seldom there when you want him - but, at any rate, it does not require a *very* great effort of the imagination to picture him slowly patrolling some weedy swim like a 'blue-robed guardian of the city's peace', and the alacrity with which the finny loafer 'moves on' at his appearance, without twice bidding, strengthens rather than otherwise the simile. Then again, when the soft south wind smites the white-mantled hills, and the water is green with snow broth, he sinks into a torpid slumber in his shaded haunt, just like the country 'peeler' who, all last winter while the snow and the slush lay on the ground making things exceeding uncomfortable outside, nightly sought the shelter of the summer-house on the lawn of a relative of mine, and in blissful slumber snored away the long weary watches of the night in the execution of his duty. But he reminds me most of all of the constable when he suddenly pokes his snout into a swim where a shoal of guileless gudgeon, or young roach, or any other small fish are innocently disporting themselves - possibly trespassing. You can almost hear them shriek "Copper!"

as they skedaddle in all directions - in all, that is, except one. Perhaps you have been an interested spectator of such a scene? If not, you can see pretty nearly the same thing almost any day in any town or city when there is snow on the ground. Look out for a quiet by-street where a gang of street arabs are sliding or snow-balling, and watch them until one of their number, more alert than the others, yells "P'leece!" That is it exactly.

But looking at the jack in this fanciful way, he doesn't seem very consistent. His character shows too many phases. There appears to be too much of the 'all things to all men' business about it. The professional housebreaker is the very antithesis to the guardian of the law, and yet in the pike the two are to some extent combined. The overshot underjaw, the low forehead and the savage gleam of the close-set eyes, all indicate the coarse brutality of a Bill Sikes. The policy of his daily life, too, is identical with that of the vulgar crib-cracker. Whatever he can lay his teeth on is his. While on this question of physiognomy there is another thing I should like to point out. I have noticed occasionally - oftenest in old pike - in the features of *Esox lucius* a sort of raffish, rorty grin. It is difficult to sketch the exact expression from memory, and I am afraid I have not succeeded very well; but I daresay you will remember having noticed it now that I mention it. It gives the wearer of it a certain 'ikey' look - the air of a 'chickaleary bloke' from the purlieus of Whitechapel or the Old Kent Road.

"Knocked 'em in the Old Kent Road"

We have by no means exhausted the multifarious disguises of our rapacious friend. He is undertaker, grave-digger, and officiating clergyman all rolled into one, and I can easily imagine him set up in business at a quiet corner near some busy thoroughfare, while outside his business premises is exhibited a sign bearing the words, 'Funerals attended to with promptitude and despatch!' (especially 'despatch'), or, perhaps still better, 'Burying done while you wait!' he is like the sexton in the old song: '*He gathers 'em in - he gathers 'em in'*.

"Gather, Gather. I Gather Them In" - The Sexton

That fancy fades and another takes its place. This time the pike has removed from the undertaker's shop, and donning the apron and cap, has set up in business as the proprietor of one of a long row of 'respectable' boarding houses, where lodgers are 'taken in and done for'.

"Just Room For One!"

But I love best to think of him as the conductor of a pirate bus. It matters not what may be the intended destinations of the unwary fish-wayfarers, in they go willy-nilly, if Jack can lay hands on them. He assists them over the step, so to speak, with more of zeal than of ceremony. They are all inside passengers and he is not particular about over-crowding his vehicle. Sometimes his enthusiasm gets the better of his caution, and he catches a Tartar, in the shape of an obstreperous passenger, who refuses to be either bullied or cajoled; but more often than not he stows his victim comfortably away, and resumes his outlook for another fare.

"A Wet Day - "Full Inside!"

A Pike, a Jack and the Pitchfork

'The Scientific Angler', The Fishing Gazette *(January, 1894)*

This story originally comes from David Foster's *The Scientific Angler* first published in 1882:

The largest pike we ever killed was taken upon a stout salmon spinning trace, the flight being mounted upon the finest gimp. We were fishing in preserved water in a neighbouring western county, and had hooked a pickerel a few odd pounds weight; when we were about to land the young gent, the gleaming broadside of some larger relation of the family shone in the background, an instant, and then a heavy tug demonstrated the fact that our possession of the prey was disputed. Comprehending the situation, we let out line with the earnest hope that this considerate exhibition of feeling would meet with due appreciation; nor were we disappointed, for after the lapse of a few minutes, which, under the circumstances it must be admitted, seemed rather long ones, the fun began.

We were in sole possession of a light punt upon an extensive sheet of water, and thus, having plenty of sea room, we were rather confident as to the result. At the first gentle touch of the rod, the fish ran out fully half-a-hundred yards of line, at one impetuous rush, despite the heavy strain placed upon the rod. A heavier reserve was now put on the remaining portion of line through the medium of the rod, but here we discovered our command over him to be considerably less than we calculated, for such was the determination of the hooked fish to explore the other side of the lake that the punt began to move in chase. To reserve the remainder of our line would tend to aggravate the nuisance, to let it run meant disaster.

Whilst we hesitated we unconsciously stopped further supply of line, of which fact we were forcibly reminded by the rapid motion of the punt as it progressed across the water.

Just as we had resolved to break away from him he suddenly doubled, making straight for the punt - we hauled in the loose line in coils at our feet as actively as was practicable under the circumstances - the next instant he dashed off with renewed vigour at right angles, and we again strained heavily upon every foot he stole, despite which our whole stock was all but spent before he again turned. For more than an hour was this operation of hauling in and paying out line repeated without ceasing, at the end of which time the final tragic end seemed as remote as ever. By this time several stable functionaries from the adjoining mansion arrived upon the scene, among whom a learned controversy ensued as to the probable weight and breed of a fish capable of towing a man and a boat with impunity. As the fish swerved along shore in their immediate proximity all dispute suddenly dropped, and we observed, what had previously escaped our notice, namely, a large stable fork in the possession of a bandy-legged individual who had stepped forward, fork in hand, ready for action. Before we could interfere a wild thrust was made, which, however, fell short of the mark, as may very easily be imagined; nevertheless it well nigh ended the fight, the terrified fish making for less dangerous quarters at a rate that eclipsed all previous exploits, the pressure upon the line availing little beyond keeping the snout of the fish above the water's surface. The winch 'whirred' loudly, not withstanding the deeply curved sturdy rod. "Hark how the d____l squeals!" exclaimed the crooked individual in possession of the fork. Had that worthy chanced to have been in the punt at that particular moment, we felt an inward presentiment that he might have suddenly found himself *out* of it. After this final rush a reaction set in, the fish showing signs of fatigue for the first time, which speedily developed into complete exhaustion. To consummate the capture by gaffing and boarding was now a very easy matter and successfully accomplished. The weight of the fish proved to be 37 3/4lb. It was preserved and cased by the owner of the water, to whom it was presented, with the tail of the pickerel protruding from its extended jaw.

How the English Record Pike was Caught

Alfred Jardine

Alfred Jardine, who though acknowledged to be the greatest pike fisherman of his time, had the tiresome habit of writing to magazines to dispute the weight of any big pike reported if its weight approached or exceeded the weight of his own two biggest fish, namely his 36 and 37lb pike. But at long last in 1894, tired of his constant tirade of insult and abuse, a few famous contemporaries, notably among them the old war horse of the Piscatorial Society E.T. Sachs took, in the columns of *The Fishing Gazette*, a closer look at Jardine's own claims, and succeeded in pinpointing some unaccountable discrepancies.

When it was pointed out, in spite of Jardine's previous insistence to the contrary, that there was no record of any 36 or 37lb pike ever having been officially weighed in - in the records of the Piscatorial Society - Jardine switched his tactics by claiming that the Shardeloes pike (the subject of the following account) was weighed in at Amersham at a weight of 37lb.

Following this rough handling, and remember that it was now December 1894, some fifteen years after he caught the Shardeloes pike, Jardine saw fit to describe the event for the first time:

One stormy afternoon in November, 1879, I set forth to fish a beautiful lake in Buckinghamshire (situated in a well-timbered park), but although it has been described as 'a pond', it was approaching twenty acres in extent, and held a good store of large pike and perch, which afforded fine sport to those lucky anglers who, through the kindness of its late owner, 'The Squire', had permission to fish there.

But to return to my own pike fishing experiences. The L. and N.W. rail took me to Rickmansworth, and after a few miles ride from thence I found myself at a comfortable old-fashioned hostelry, on the high road to Aylesbury and Buckingham, noted in former coaching days. My first care was to look to my live baits (some dozens of Thames dace). Accordingly a stable-lad was requisitioned, who carried them to a little stream which flows through the town, and I placed the cans with the baits in running water; then back to the inn, where the landlord had a roast hen pheasant ready and waiting me for my supper.

As I have said, the weather was stormy, and when I got to bed sleep was well-nigh impossible, for fierce gusts of wind shook the old house, and rattled the casements. Against my window the boughs of an old pear tree swayed and scraped, and the signboard of the inn swung and 'scrooped' on its rusty hinges to such an extent that I had only fitful sleep, between the intervals dreaming of huge pike; but with the first dawn of day-break I dressed and got to the brook, where I found my bait cans undisturbed, and the dace alive and strong. By nine o'clock I was on my way to the lake, where my old friend, Mr W. H. Brougham, of the Thames Angling Preservation Society, had promised to join me about noon. I therefore told the landlord to send on our lunch by the waggonette which would bring my friend. The keeper was waiting my arrival, and considered it useless to fish, as the gale blowing along the lake was lashing its surface into waves of some size, and, moreover, both punts were sunk at their moorings; but as I have always found big pike to lose their habitual caution and feed well in rough weather, I decided to fish, and, with the aid of an under keeper, we dragged up and baled-out the smaller punt, built Thames fashion, with a well to contain the live baits, and, getting afloat, it took me nearly half an hour to row up the lake in the face of such a tempest, for I elected to first 'spin' the shallows over, where the stream comes in at the top end. On my voyage I shipped much water, but at last got anchored stern-on to the wind, made a commencement, and soon found my spinning flight and dace completely covered with green slime, which took a lot of time and trouble to clean off, and which recurred so constantly that I shifted to deeper water, tried paternoster, and live-bait snap fishing, sliming and killing many baits, but not capturing a solitary pike. On 'sampling' the water in a tumbler, I found it was full of fine green filaments that had been broken by the billows from the masses of silk-weed, which grew luxuriantly on the shallow waters of the lake. I therefore made another move to a position more sheltered from the gale by some trees growing on an island, because I had a lively recollection that near this spot in September, 1878, a tremendous tussle took place between a very big pike and the late Mr T. S. Spreckley, while Mr Brougham and I were fishing with him; but the pike after some minutes' play 'severed the connection', and made off with bait, tackle and float, leaving Mr Spreckley with a broken rod and line, and his equanimity much disturbed.

An elm, blown over by previous winter storms, lay in the lake, its roots still fixed to the edge of the island, and among its submerged branches was the haunt and vantage place of this big pike. I fixed my punt close in to the opposite shore, so as to fish round about the tree, where the water was some 8 feet deep, and used a large dace on snap-tackle.

It was an easy cast of about thirty yards into a clear channel between the weeds, and there I left my bait to play about, while with another rod I worked a spinning bait all over the water near. In less than ten minutes my check-winch gave a screech, for the pike had taken my dace, and was making for the waterlogged tree, when I caught up the rod and 'drove home the steel'. The fish rushed for the open water, taking out nearly 100 yards of line from the reel, then leaped clear above the surface of the lake, its dimensions showing me that I had hooked Mr Spreckley's pike. My tackle was good, and held fast; but with that modesty which does or should pertain to anglers, I will pass over the details of the conflict. It suffices to say that, after a 'battle royal' of half an hour or so, I had the pike alongside, my gaff tucked into its under jaw, and the fish safe in my punt.

I then rowed over to the island, and anchored on a bed of sedges cut off a foot under water, lit my pipe, and after admiring my capture, wrapped it in my mackintosh, and placed it close alongside the well, with its head and tail bent up, for the fish was nearly a foot longer than the width of the punt.

The keeper, who had been to feed his pheasants, then appeared, and asked me from across the lake if I had met with any luck, for on such a tempestuous morning he almost expected, he said, to find the punt upset, with me overboard or drowned. I told him the only pike I had caught was over 5lb, and therefore of retainable size. He thought it was fortunate I had saved 'a blank', and had a fish to take home. I asked him to get help to raise and bale out the other punt, and then to come to me, for I wanted a talk, my pipe, and whisky. Consequently in about twenty minutes he rowed alongside, between me and the island. I asked him to step into my punt and sit on the well, and to stretch out his legs so as not to tread on my mackintosh.

Then I began to tell him of my bad night's sleep, how I dreamt someone had captured his big pike. "Oh, no," he said; "nobody has caught it, for I saw the fish only yesterday 'full on the feed', just about where we are now - its home is under that tree which has fallen into the water. It is that big pike that smashed up your friend, Mr Spreckley, also Mr Lukin, and our Squire's brother (the rector), and many other anglers. People do say there are enough hooks in its jaws to stock a tackle shop."

"Well," I said, "I did not believe there was such a fish in the water." Then I told him I dreamt he had picked up a sovereign. "Ah," he replied, "I never did that but once; it was in our churchyard, but the coin was a bad one, worse luck."

"Bollinger," I said, "don't you think it's time you had a whisky and a smoke. Turn over my mackintosh, and inside it you will find a cigar I just now dropped." He did so, and jumped up, exclaiming, "But what's this!" I said, "It is your big pike; I have caught it, and my dream has come true, and here (handing it to him) pick up your sovereign." "Mr Jardine," he said, "there is another pike as large in the lake, come and catch that." "No," I said, "quantum sufficit; this one contents me; I shall fish no more today."

Neither did I. Then came the waggonette bringing Mr Brougham and our lunch. So Bollinger rowed across to a sloping, gravelly bank, close by a large oak tree. My friend seated himself on the stern locker, and inquired what sport I had had, "For," said he, "on the road to Rickmansworth, I met the Squire, who told me that as he drove through the park, he saw you on the lake, shipping lots of water, and with very little prospect (he thought) of catching fish in such stormy weather." "Well," I replied, "I have caught one, and only one, but it is of retainable size." "Ah," said W.H.B., "you always were a lucky angler."

The keeper arranged two boards across the punt, and on these spread our lunch, which I remember consisted of a roast loin of delicate country pork, with the proper adjuncts, and a bottle of old brown sherry.

I faced my friend and we 'fell to' at our meal. Lunch over, W.H.B. wanted to see my capture, so I said, "Step ashore, and you shall." But, while he was doing this, I lifted the pike out of my mackintosh, and placed it on the seat he had just vacated. He turned round, saw the pike, and had such a surprise, he was all but speechless, but just able to ask for a dram of whiskey to 'steady his nerves'. "Why," I said, "you have just had half a bottle of sherry; you will be 'tight'." However, the whisky did him good, and he wished me to continue fishing; but, no, that one fish was all I needed, and I passed the next few hours in pleasant chat with my old friend and Bollinger (the keeper), and

Our afternoon ended, the horse we did make fast,
And went in the waggonette back to our breakfast.

I mean we went to our dinner, but that does not rhyme. The pike was weighed in the village, and just turned 37lb. Next morning I took it to the studio in Nicholas Lane, E.C., of the late H.L. Rolfe, and left it there until the following day, while he painted its portrait for the centre-piece of the large fish picture, presented by anglers to the Right Hon. Anthony Mundella, M.P., in recognition of his services in getting the Freshwaters Fisheries Act passed through Parliament, and forty-eight hours after capture the big pike weighed within a shade of 35lb on the scales of the Piscatorial Society.

> Unfortunately for poor old Jardine, M.W. H. Brougham (the companion who joined him for lunch) although dead by 1894, had left a note (in *The Fishing Gazette*, 22nd November, 1879) regarding their attempt to get the fish weighed at Amersham.

On arriving in the quaint old country town [Amersham], which was over a mile distant from the water, we ordered our coachman to drive up to the butcher's to have the fish weighed; but we were told they could weigh nothing over 30lb, which the fish, on being tried, easily overbalanced . . . On arriving in London Mr Jardine took his fish to the Piscatorial Society to be weighed, and after being out of the water for twelve hours, it scaled 34¾lb, so that it was a good 36lb fish, and a remarkably handsome specimen. On the following morning it was on view at Mr Jardine's office; *and in contrast with the other 35lb fish* [my italics] which he caught under similar circumstances two years ago, there was not a pin to choose which was the best fish.

The Demon Pike of Sparshott Lake

Major W.G. Turle, The Fishing Gazette *(16th December, 1893)*

"One, two, three. One, two, three; no, that's wrong again. However is one to read music with the time changing every minute, I should like to know?" exclaimed a young girl, turning impatiently away from the worn out jingling piano, and apostrophising the old walls of the quaint morning room at Sparshott Manor. Everything around her was more or less antique, from the heavy oak beams across the ceiling to the worm-eaten boards of the floor. The Sparshotts of Sparshott were old-fashioned folk, and kept the place very much the same as it had been handed down to them by their forefathers, they had not ambition nor money enough to enable them to be up to our present rapid luxurious date.

The musician had hardly settled herself down to another try at the baffling score, when her further study was broken off by the hurried intrusion of a portly middle-aged woman.

"Marian," she said abruptly, "where is your sister?"

"How you do startle one, mother," cried the girl petulantly, as she swung herself round on the music stool. "Where is Amy," she repeated in an aggrieved tone; "why out on the lake with Mr Plimansol, of course, as usual - look for yourself," and she pointed through the window across the smooth lawn, to where the gently shelving banks joined a wide expanse of water. On the calm smiling bosom of the lake, by the light of the pale December sun, a boat containing two persons was distinctly visible.

"All right," replied Mrs Sparshott, hurrying away. But, before she could reach the door, Marian burst out -

"Oh, you call it all right, do you? I should say it was all wrong. Since Jack brought his precious friend here, Amy has been just good for nothing. It is too bad the way he monopolises her. She promised to try these duets with me this morning, and now she has gone and forgotten all about them. You ought not to allow it."

Mrs Sparshott was too accustomed to her daughter's pettishness to take much notice of it, though she could not help smiling to herself as she beat a hasty retreat at the idea of her interfering between the lover and his lass. Had she not been hoping and praying for years that one of her daughters might be blessed with a well-to-do, good-looking, thoroughly honest young fellow for a husband? - and Lawrence Plimansol was all that.

Ten days ago the young people were strangers, and if Jack Sparshott had not brought his chum to spend Christmas at the old manor, Lawrence and Amy might never have met. And now they are all and all to each other. Amy, as she lazily steered the boat clear of the tall brown faded reeds on this bright winter morning, felt as if her cup of happiness was full. On the other hand, Lawrence, though an ardent lover, was also an enthusiastic fisherman.

"What an awfully jolly lake this is of yours," he remarked, resting on his oars a minute in order to contemplate the water, "and what noble fish there are in it. Just look at that grand old man swimming majestically along; he is a real patriarch amongst pike. I never saw such a big fellow, and the expression on his ugly old mug is absolutely diabolical. He must be a fifty-pounder if he is an ounce. Wouldn't I like to have a hook in him." A half-stifled cry from his companion made him look up quickly, "Amy, what is the matter?" he asked in alarm, as the young girl uttered an exclamation of dismay, and turned very pale.

"Row on, Lawrence, quick!" she cried in great agitation, "don't look down, it will bring you misfortune; it must be the demon fish."

"What do you mean?" he inquired, much exercised in his mind for the young girl's distress was too genuine for him to believe it possible she could be joking. "There! It's gone now," he added, in the hope of reassuring her. Amy breathed again.

"Really?" she said anxiously.

"Honour bright! But, Amy," he continued, "why did you call it a demon fish?"

"I wish you had not noticed it," she sighed, "something is sure to go wrong now, ill luck always follows those who see it."

"But, my darling," expostulated the practical lover, "you don't mean to say you believe there is an evil spirit inhabiting the lake?"

"Well, perhaps not that exactly," she returned, gravely nodding her curly head, "but they tell strange stories about the demon pike, and some of them I know are true. It has been in the lake ever so long. They say it was seen basking in the moonlight the night our great, great, grandfather was shot by a highwayman, and that was more than one hundred and fifty years ago. Whenever any misfortune befalls the village, the demon is certain to be seen basking, generally when the moon is full. But at other times it lies hidden in the holes, which are numerous and deep."

"But, Amy," interposed the experienced angler,

"this is downright nonsense, pike don't live a hundred and fifty years or bask in the moonlight."

"I dare say ordinary pike do not, but this is an extraordinary one, as I told you before. If you think I am talking nonsense, I had better leave off," rejoined Amy, in rather an injured tone of voice.

"No; go on to the bitter end," answered Lawrence resignedly; "but how is it that no one has tried to rid the lake of this evil monster?"

"Lots of people have done so, but they nearly all came to a bad end, being mostly drowned, and when taken out of the water each one presented the same appearance of laceration on one leg, as if they had been seized and dragged down by some huge creature with awfully sharp teeth. This I know for a fact, papa's little brother went out fishing one day against his parents' express command, and was drowned. And I remember papa saying that, when the poor child's body was recovered, the left leg showed signs of having been terribly mangled."

"How horrible!" exclaimed Lawrence, impressed in spite of himself.

"And grandmamma," Amy went on, almost too engrossed in her story to notice her lover's involuntary ejaculation, "told how the boy, the day before his death, had talked excitedly about the big fish he had seen in the lake. There is not a villager who would willingly, in his sober senses, go near the lake after dark," she continued confidently. "But belated wayfarers, under the influence of public-house beer, have from time to time come home with the story of how they saw a monster pike lying on the surface of the water in the moonlight. One man goes so far as to declare that it opened a huge pair of crocodile-like jaws and closed them with such a terrific snap that he fled away in mortal terror. It is a well-known fact that he was found next morning, wet and shivering, more dead than alive between two hatch holes in the neighbouring river, where he had passed the night in fear and trembling, dreading to move lest he should tumble in and be drowned right out."

"I wonder under the circumstances you don't have the water drained off, and the holes filled up, and so get rid of the brute," remarked Lawrence. The tone of sarcasm in which he spoke was entirely lost upon Amy, who replied simply.

"The scheme has often been talked of, but it costs money, not easily to be spared in these bad times. Besides, there is a general belief about here that some dire disaster would fall upon the village if the demon were to be meddled with." On which her companion could not help observing, that there seemed to be a good deal of superstition left in the country, in spite of Board Schools and County Councils.

"And do you," he began incredulously, "an educated woman, believe that, in spite of all the laws of nature, a pike can live for over a hundred and fifty years, and cherish a murderous hatred against the whole human race?"

"I assert nothing," replied Amy a little stiffly, for she did not like the tradition, in which she had been brought up, being treated with ridicule; "but," she concluded shrewdly, "you yourself must allow there is a monster fish in the lake."

"Yes, he was certainly a whopper," Lawrence felt bound to admit, "though I dare say I was deceived as to his real size. However, I mean to have him out before many days are over, and then we shall know to an ounce how big he is." Amy started, and again the frightened look came into her face.

"Leave it alone!" she cried piteously, her pride, her hurt feelings all flung to the winds in fear for her lover, "as you value our happiness have nothing to do with that fish. For my sake Lawrence, for my sake," she implored, bending forward and looking up at him beseechingly. The boat was small, and Amy by her sudden movement brought her pretty face into such dangerous proximity to that of her companion, that he felt himself constrained to impart a hearty kiss on the sweet parted lips.

"Oh, Lawrence!" cried the confused girl reproachfully, drawing herself back, "how could you? Don't you know that they can see us from the house."

"And what if they do," rejoined the brave lover, "they will only have the pleasure of beholding two very happy beings, eh, darling?"

"Well, you mustn't do it again. And as it is just lunch time, I should like to go home and put myself tidy," and so Lawrence very unwillingly had to row his betrothed ashore.

"There he is again! - the big fish!" he exclaimed as he tied the boat to the landing stage; "he is huge and no mistake."

"Come away, come away!" she entreated, hastening up the garden path; and he, being unwilling to cause her unnecessary distress, obeyed. "Mind," she said warningly, as they approached the house, "you must say nothing at home about seeing the great fish."

In consequence of not being allowed to speak of it, Lawrence found himself pondering much over the big pike, until at last he felt his happiness would be incomplete unless he could become possessed of such a grand specimen. His visit might, however, have terminated without his discovering any ways or means to obtain his prize if Jack Sparshott had not come to his aid.

"Amy tells me you have seen the demon this morning," began the latter, "and she is in an awful state about it; thinks you are going to glory straight off."

"You don't believe in the legend?"

"I? Rather not," returned dare-devil Jack, who feared nothing. "But the belief in the demon pike is a religious creed in our family. Did you really see an enormous fish?"

"Never came across such a creature before," Lawrence asserted confidently. Jack's eyes sparkled.

"It would be a sin and a shame not to have a try for him," he returned meditatively. "What say you?"

"I am game for anything," said Lawrence. To fish for him openly in the day time they both agreed was out of the question, as such a course would probably bring the whole household about their ears. Under cover of darkness could they alone hope to escape detection; therefore, as their time was short and their spirits impatient, they resolved to execute their nefarious designs that very night. When the lights were out and all was quiet, the two conspirators held conclave in Jack's room, and then, opening the window softly, Lawrence, who was a light weight, slight and agile, swung himself down by the branches of a big wisteria that grew close under the window. Jack then handed him the fishing tackle, and then followed suit himself.

It was bright moonlight, and as they stepped across the lawn, except for the intense cold, they might have thought it was day. Their plan was to set trimmers bated with kittens, a supply of which Jack had been fortunately able to secure from a kitchen pail, to which watery grave a stony-hearted cook had consigned the tiny helpless creatures.

Their operations completed, the young fellows crept home again to await results. No sooner had daylight set in than down they went to the lake.

"Stop a moment," said Lawrence on the way, "my boot-lace is broken. I must go back and fetch another."

"Oh, bother!" rejoined impatient Jack, "your boot will do all right as it is; it isn't as if you were going to walk ten miles." And Lawrence, always ready to oblige, went on, feeling very uncomfortable, for he was neat and careful about his dress and hated untidiness.

Together the friends loosened the boat from its moorings, and rowed out to inspect the trimmers. Even from a distance they could see these were not bobbing up and down sufficiently for them to take the flattering unction to their souls that any fish of unusual size was on. And so it turned out for the largest they hauled in would scarcely have turned the scale at a dozen pounds. This was distinctly disappointing, and the fishermen's spirits sank lower and lower as they approached the last trimmer. Just as Lawrence knelt over to take it up, his attention was attracted by some creature dark and solid, lying motionless some distance down. Suddenly it turned, and disclosed the ugliest, biggest, wickedest pike's head he had ever set eyes on. The hideous sight so astonished him, that he let the line drop out of his hand, and in his efforts to regain it, fell over the side of the boat, headlong into the water. Next moment he reappeared, swimming valorously, at some little distance from the boat. All at once, without apparent rhyme or reason, he flung up his arms, and disappeared.

Thereupon, before the eyes of the amazed and horrified Jack, the calm surface of the placid lake seemed lashed up into violent agitation just at the spot where his friend had so mysteriously vanished.

Jack Sparshott was not an imaginative fellow, but he said afterwards that it was the rummiest go he had ever seen, and gave him quite a turn. He did not, however, allow himself much time to think, and dashing off boots, coat, and waistcoat plunged into the icy cold water to the rescue. The cause of the commotion ceased as quickly as it had arisen and Lawrence, pale and exhausted, rose once more to the surface. On this, Jack promptly caught the inanimate form in his stout arms, and swam with it back to the boat. By dint of much rubbing and manual exertion, he succeeded in restoring the half-drowned man to something like animation. This accomplished, he wrapped the patient up in his own dry coat, and made for shore as quickly as possible; then taking his charge in his burly arms he carried him up to the house, where their deplorable appearance naturally caused general consternation.

Under Mrs Sparshott's motherly care, Lawrence rapidly recovered, though she insisted on keeping him a semi-invalid for the rest of the day, condemning him to a comfortable sofa in the morning room with Amy for his attendant, an arrangement against which neither of them felt inclined to rebel. The account he gave of his accident was not very explanatory, he only knew that, as he was swimming towards the boat, something seemed to grasp hold of one of his legs and drag him down, and whilst he was struggling to get free the weight suddenly dropped off. After that he remembered no more till he found himself in the boat again.

Next morning the gentlemen were to shoot the coverts, when Lawrence, now fully himself again, discovered one of his shooting boots was missing. Search was made in all likely and unlikely places, with the upshot that he had to start off in another less suitable pair.

"Was it the boot that you had on yesterday with the broken lace?" inquired Jack.

"Yes."

"Then I think you will have to go to the bottom of the lake to find it, as you had only one on when I hauled you out of the water."

A short time after the events just related, the keeper presented himself to Mr Sparshott one morning, saying as how he had found in shallow water, near a deep hole in the lake, an extraordinary large dead pike. He described the head as being four times the size of that of an ordinary fish, and what was more astonishing, tight wedged between its formidable jaws it held a thick shooting boot. The gentlemen ought to come and see it, which the gentlemen did without loss of time.

There it lay on the bank, dead through its own stupid ferocity, a perfect mammoth amongst pike, measuring fully five feet long, with its enormous jaws stuck fast in the cause of its destruction.

"Why it is the identical boot I have been looking for everywhere," exclaimed Lawrence in extreme surprise. "That then is what I felt tugging at my foot."

"Lucky for you that the lace was broken, or you might not have got free from the jaws of the savage brute so easily," observed his friend.

"No, I was pretty well spent when you came to the rescue, old boy; another minute would have done for me."

The villagers, of course, all came to stare at the dead monster, but the question as to whether it was the real demon pike or not is still an open question to this day. The dead fish's head showed it to be old, very old, upwards of seventy years, experts said - much more than the allotted span of pike life. But then the demon, to have accorded with all the legions about it, must have had an existence of nearly double that period. So folks argued for and against, as they met in the comfortable village clubhouse of a winter's evening, all agreeing, however, that since the finding of the big fish, that choked itself with Mr Lawrence's boot, the demon was never seen again. At the same time there are a few old people who believe he is still lurking in one of the holes at the bottom of Sparshott Lake.

Another English Record Pike

Clifford Warwick, Angling Times *(9th April, 1954)*

Colonel Martin Baker and I were staying with my old friend, Mr Mitchell-Hedges, the famous big game fisherman, at his place at Fordingbridge. On his two-mile stretch of the Hampshire Avon we had fished the previous day and caught a plentiful supply of live-bait. It was a perfect morning in the first week of October and on arrival at the bank of the river not a ripple broke the surface.

While fishing for roach and dace the day before we had seen several big pike striking and the scales, which floated to the surface, told a tale of havoc caused among the shoals.

So with high hopes we unmoored the punt and drifted downstream above five hundred yards and lowered the weight anchor. Each using a roach weighing fully 1lb as live-bait, we gently cast out the lively fish - and lively they were, for almost at once both our floats disappeared, coming to the surface, then bobbing down again and again.

Several times it looked like a run. Within twenty yards of the punt a big fish struck - a burst of water and small fish flew in every direction. Our expectations were keyed to the highest pitch and every moment we expected a strike, but fully half an hour went by and our baits, still working strongly, remained untouched.

Then suddenly the Colonel's float went down, the line ran off the reel, he struck and was fast into a fish. After playing for a matter of a few minutes he brought to the side of the punt a pike about 10lb, which we carefully unhooked and placed in the well of the boat.

Another hour went by without a strike so we unanchored and drifted down the river to just below where another stream entered.

In the meantime nothing had touched my bait. It would seem it was my unlucky day. The Colonel was having a grand sport, for having rebaited, his float had not drifted down more than 20 feet from the boat when down it went. He struck and the line was torn off the reel at a terrific speed.

The fish made for mid-stream, circled and for twenty-five minutes put up a really game fight but the Colonel was no beginner. Playing it carefully he finally brought alongside a magnificent clean fish weighing just over 22lb. He was chuckling quietly to himself.

I admit that I was getting somewhat nettled. Here the Colonel had caught four fish and up till now, I had not had a single touch. I slowly reeled my bait in, detached it from the hook and rebaited with the largest roach I could find in the well, it must have weighed quite $1^1/_2$ lb. The Colonel had laid his rod down and was still chuckling at my discomfiture.

"Go on, laugh away," I said, "just wait and see," and I dropped the bait close to the side of the boat.

"You won't get one there," advised the Colonel but the words were hardly out of his mouth before the float disappeared and there was a tremendous pull on the line.

Twenty, thirty, forty yards were torn off the reel. I put on as much pressure as I dared but still could not stop the rush. Over seventy yards of line had disappeared when the fish turned, shot across to the opposite side of the river, and swam upstream at a tremendous pace.

As the line hissed through the water in a wide arc we were treated to a most extraordinary sight. The pace of the fish was so great that the line cut through the long weeds deep down exactly like a scythe and masses floated to the surface.

Both Mitchell-Hedges and the Colonel, standing up in the punt, were greatly excited.

Doggedly the fish continued upstream, but fortunately I had a hundred yards of line on the reel and when I was really worried that the end might be reached, the fish turned. Downstream it came, again as fast as ever.

The strength of the fish seemed inexhaustible. Over half an hour had gone by since it was first hooked and there was no sign yet of weakening. I had over eighty yards of line out when the fish appeared to stop and commenced to bore sullenly but almost stationary. I tried to regain a few yards but it was impossible.

Suddenly the fish turned and shot straight in towards the punt. I reeled in the slack as hard as I could and when almost up to the boat it sheered off at right angles towards the opposite bank and again travelled upstream.

"Look out, Cliff," roared the Colonel, for the fish was close in to where a big willow tree hung over the river with its lower branches actually in the water. I risked everything and put every ounce of strain I dared on the line, for I knew that if the fish made those submerged tangled branches a smash was certain. But he missed it by inches, turned and again travelled downstream past the end of the punt and came to the surface.

But I could feel now the fish was certainly weakening and I really had hopes. Slowly but surely I brought it closer to the boat.

Slowly I brought him back from underneath the boat and to the surface close alongside. Mitchell-Hedges bent over, and, getting both his hands underneath the fish, raised it carefully like a baby, and deposited it on the floor of the punt.

Mitchell-Hedges swore it was the English record. The Colonel was dubious and so was I, and we argued all the time as we poled the punt upstream to the landing place.

Removing the pike from the well of the punt we discovered it had disgorged a breakfast weighing over 4lb. It consisted of an eel, roach and a water rat. The last could have only very recently been swallowed as there was no sign of digestion and the fur was in perfect condition.

We now all felt very doubtful that the fish would be a record, but, however, on weighing it, it turned the scales at 37½ lb. The fish, a female, was in perfect condition, its length was 49 inches and girth 24½ inches.

Pike Attack

Frederick Buller

The sixteenth century story of the Polish girl whose foot was bitten while she was washing clothes is definitive background for the student of pike voracity. It originates from *The Compleat Angler*, although Walton got his information from the German author Gesner. In another incident during the sixteenth century, Killingworth Pond, not far from Coventry, also produced a pike that bit a maiden's foot. Familiarity with this oft repeated story, which is usually quoted in some humorous context, could breed a contempt for the pike's human biting proclivities, which could in turn lull the reader into complete disbelief of the pike's capacity to repeat the exercise.

There is much evidence for the pike's occasional attack on parts of the human anatomy. I have a photograph, which depicts the evidence of a musky bite suffered by an American, that will quickly dispel the joke aspect of pike bites - or it will for those whose bare bodies are exposed in waters known to harbour large specimens of the pike family. The North American musky or muskellunge generally grows to a larger size than its cousin the northern pike. Judging by the bite mark on the angler's calf I think the musky would have weighed at least 40lb.

In 1829 a Dr Genzik, when a student at Vienna, witnessed an attack on a fellow student (later Dr Gouge - a celebrated surgeon):

We all plunged in immediately to his rescue, and succeeded in bringing him to the surface, and finally in getting him up on to the hoarding of the bath, when a pike was found sticking fast to his right heel, which would not loose its hold, but was killed, and eaten by us all in company the same evening. It weighed 32lb. Gouge suffered for months from the bite.

Innish Owen, a fishing correspondent of *The Fishing Gazette* wrote in 1898:

In the river Barrow, near Carlow, a pike attacked a man, who was shovelling gravel out of the river. The man killed it with a blow of the shovel. It weighed 36lb. The man had to be removed to the infirmary, as the calf of his leg had been severely gashed by this medium-sized pike.

The *Swiss Times* of 1874 printed a literal translation of a paragraph that had just appeared in *Feuille d'Avis*, of Neuchatel:

Some days ago a boy of twelve or thirteen years of age, who was bathing in the Cret, and not far from the bank, was the victim of an accident happily rare in our lake. All at once he felt himself seized by the leg and drawn under water; believing himself to be the object of some pleasantry on the part of a comrade, he combated his opponent, came to the surface and what was his fright to see disappear, instead of a human form, a dark mass, which it would seem was nothing else than a large pike. This at least is the only solution which an inspection of the wounds on the leg of the boy would seem to offer.

The Daily Telegraph in 1979 told a story of an attack on a dog:

A seven-stone Alsatian guard dog was recovering with seven stitches in his leg yesterday after being bitten by a pike while swimming in a lake at Sudbury, Derbyshire. He had been taken for his daily walk around the lake by Mr Tony Wright, landlord of the Vernon Arms, Sudbury.

Barney, aged 3, was swimming when a pike grabbed his hind leg and tried to pull him under. Mr Wright managed to pull the dog to the side of the lake, with the fish still clinging to his leg. Eventually the pike slid off into the water.

Mr Wright said yesterday:

It was only the dog's strength that prevented him being pulled under. Barney had to struggle against the pike, it was huge, a smaller dog would most certainly have drowned'.

And from the *Daily Mirror* in 1978:

A pet dog jumped into a lake to retrieve a stick - and became a meal for a monster pike. Fiona Dick, 14, watched in horror as her 17-month-old Cairn terrier, Hamish, was dragged backwards into the depths of the lake. Now parents have been warned to keep small children and pets out of the lake at Chipstead, Kent.

The local angling society says 40lb pike haunt the lake, and adds:

These fish have attacked foxes, so I'm afraid a little terrier would be just a snack for one of them.

The headline below heralded a piece in *The Evening News* in 1921:

Girl Attacked by Giant Pike

Gripped in Jaws of Fierce Fish while Bathing and Held Like a Vice

A girl was fiercely attacked by a giant jack (pike)

while bathing in Frensham Pond, Surrey, today. The girl - Miss Shallis - selected a secluded spot to bathe in, and when she entered the water the great fish, darting from its haunt, seized her by the leg and held her like a vice.

The more she struggled the tighter became the hold. Exhausted by pain and fright the girl finally sank in the water.

At that moment other bathers, attracted by her cries, arrived at the spot, and the monster fish, lashing the water, relinquished his hold and vanished.

Miss Shallis's leg was badly lacerated.

Very large pike weigh about 30lb and have very large jaws. Usually when disturbed in the water they swim away.

In December 1981 I received a letter from John Cameron from Beeston, Notts, drawing my attention to *The Daily Telegraph* of 25th August, 1981:

Cycle Race Chief Killed by Fish Bite

M. Claude Gaillard, 55, Commissioner of the Tour de France, died last Saturday at La Roche sur Yon, from a virus infection contracted after he was bitten by a fish.

M. Gaillard, who was on holiday, was bitten by a pike while fishing in a river near the village of Chaille les Marais a week ago. He was taken to hospital on Friday after he developed a fever.

Experts said the virus, leptospirosis, may have come from the water. The commonest carriers are sewer rats and pigs.

Mr Cameron went on to say:

My mother-in-law, who lives only 15 miles from La Roche, wrote to my wife and told her to make sure that I was careful whilst pike fishing or the same could happen to me. I replied that it was such a rare occurrence that I had more chance of getting hit on the head by a meteor than being killed by a pike.

And finally the best authenticated account of attempted manslaughter by a pike! The attack occurred on a comparatively recent date, in June 1856, in Surrey. The particulars were given by in the *Reading Mercury* and are as follows:

A lad aged fifteen, named Longhurst, had gone into Inglemere Pond, near Ascot Heath, to bathe, and when he had walked in to the depth of about four feet, a huge fish, supposed to be a pike, suddenly rose to the surface and seized his hand. The pike, finding himself resisted, abandoned the boy's hand, but still followed, and caught hold of his other hand, which he bit very severely. The lad, clenching the hand which had been first bitten, struck his assailant a heavy blow on the head, upon which the fish swam away. A local surgeon, W. Barr Brown, dressed seven wounds, two of which were very deep, and which bled profusely.

A few days after this occurrence, a woodsman was walking by the side of the pond, when he saw something white floating in it. A man, who was passing on horseback, rode in, and found it to be a large pike in a dying state; he twisted his whip round it and brought it to shore.

The boy who was attacked was immediately sent for to look at it, and at once recognised his antagonist. The fish appeared to have been a long time in the agonies of death; and the body was very lean, and curved like a bow. It measured 41 inches, and died the next day, and, I believe, was taken to the Castle at Windsor.

> There can be no doubt, that this fish was in a state of complete starvation . . . If well-fed, it is probable it might have weighed between 30 to 40lb.

Giant Pike and How They Get Weighed

George Thorne

George Thorne of Broxbourne, the inventor of an early pike length/weight scale wrote:

It seems almost a cruelty to dispel the fond illusions that pike exist of weight and dimensions far beyond any yet set up by Cooper [J. Cooper & Sons the famous firm of Taxidermists]. All I can say is my faith has been rudely shaken. The following is a curious coincidence: 'Blatherwicke' quotes Buckland: 'On the steamer which runs from Galway to Cong a gentleman told me that a man had caught a pike in Lough Cong (sic! query Corrib) which he himself had seen weighed, and it turned the beam at 47lb'. Now, Mr Editor, there is only one steamer that ever plied between Galway and Cong that I am aware of. Some years ago in that very steamer I interviewed the captain. My object was information about big pike.

I was off piking up the lough, and the conversation became fishy. I asked the captain what size was the biggest pike he had ever heard of in Lough Corrib. Answer: "The biggest pike ever heard of in these parts we picked up on this lough. It was choked, sir, trying to swallow a 9lb salmon. We saw it floundering on the lough, stopped the steamer, and picked it up. The salmon weighed 9lb, sir, and the pike weighed 48lb." Mr Editor, I was almost a believer, yet still in doubt. Now the engineer was a most intelligent man; we had many a yarn together; he had driven the engines from the time the boat was launched. I interviewed the engineer. "Oh, yes, sorr, I remember the big pike; he was choked, sorr, trying to swallow a 9lb salmon." "Yes, but how much did the pike weigh? Didn't you weigh the pike?" "Yes, sorr, sure it weighed 35lb, sorr, bumping weight."

A 60lb pike. - Some few years ago *The Field* gave an account of a 60lb pike picked up dead on the shores of Lough Mask, County Mayo. The head was cut off and taken by a gentleman to London for preservation. Now, Mr Editor, I ferreted about Lough Mask; found the fisherman, one John Somers, who picked up this 60lb pike. Questioned him. Did it weigh 60lb? "Oh yes, sorr quite 60lb." I doubted. I don't believe there was a steel yard or a pair of scales within twenty miles of the place. "How did you weigh it, Somers?" "Well, sorr, this is how we weigh big pike. You know, sorr, that a man can just hold out 56lb at arm's length, and the strongest of us could hardly hold up this fish, it was so heavy." This is how big pike are weighed in some parts of Ireland. Why, Mr Editor, 'Sandow' would be rather proud of being able to hold 60lb at arm's length. I expect the Kenmure pike was measured on much the same principle.

Is it not then possible for pike to exceed 40lb in weight? I believe it is. I also believe that the average weight of a full-grown pike is 35lb, but as there are giants among men even to seven or eight feet in height, seen once in a generation, so there are giants among pike; but they are as few and far between, and the chances of their being caught or even seen are small indeed.

There may be a simple explanation to equate both accounts. Picture the scene - a steamer, *The Maid of Colerain* or its predecessor, stopping in the middle of the lough to retrieve the white-sided floating body of the pike and its entrapped victim. Imagine the crowd of curious trippers pressing forward so as to witness the cause of the stoppage. After much groping, a boathook, wielded by a crewman, lodges in the pike's gill and the fish is brought alongside and then heaved on to the deck.

In case it is still alive he bludgeons the aggressor with the handle of the boathook, making the squeamish turn their backs, but the pike's quivering fins reveal the wisdom of the precaution.

A walking stick proffered by an onlooker is passed through the pike's gills nailing it to the deck as the mate - holding the salmon's tail - pulls it from the pike's rasping-jaw.

After most of the crowd disperses the pike is weighed at thirty-five and the salmon at nine pounds. An aggregate weight of forty-four pounds. The small increase of four pounds is the kind of increase we would expect in the weight of a pike after death!

Big Pike

Frederick Buller

There can be no doubt that big pike exist; but just how big may be open to question. The following all give glimpses of what monsters have been sighted.

The Lost Sixty Pounder

'Hibernicus', *The Fishing Gazette* (24th September, 1887)

As I was trolling in a tributary to Lough Conn with a large spoon attached to a strong salmon rod by a good salmon line, a monster seized my bait so much below the surface that I only saw a wave, but no break. Instantly he snatched as if turning, and the suddenness and force of the check broke off the connection at the end of the line, and 'I was left lamenting'. I thought little of the incident after some days, until about a fortnight or three weeks had elapsed, and when shooting wild duck, I encountered in the rushes the remains of the body of a monster pike, the stench of which was insufferable. About half the carcase was consumed (unfortunately the head and shoulders), else I should have sent the same as a sample to your office, after cleaning and preparing it for transmission. I am sure I should have gained the £5 you offered for a pike over 50lb weight if I had captured this fish. The weight and force of the drag he gave my line would have convinced any experienced angler of his unusual size; but the mangled remains which were left either by the eels or by his unnatural kinsfolk were conclusive proof that he must have been over 60lb at least. This unusual circumstance, unprecedented in my experience at all events, may excite the doubts and cavils of some of your readers; but they may rely on the accuracy of the statement, which can be corroborated by an English gentleman who was present, and can vouch for its truth if necessary'. I am, &c.

The following description of a big pike caught on a trimmer appeared in *The Fishing Gazette* (13th October, 1888), and was signed by 'The Idle Esox'.

The 56lb Pike - Caught on a Frog

'The Idle Esox'

As to Irish pike, I was told by the woodman of Lieut. Col. Hoole, of Ravenfield Park, Mr Rotherham, that some years since he went to cut wood on an estate near to Lough Erne. They had to row across the lake, and hearing of the size of the fish in its waters, he baited one of the old-fashioned pike hooks with a frog, fastened it to a rough line bought in Enniskillen, and in lieu of a cork, used a piece of deal a foot square, moored it with a bit of iron and left it. It was missed for three days, when, rowing home one evening, the white deal was seen below the surface; it was recovered, and to it was hooked a big pike, nearly dead; when it was weighed it fetched the scale at more than 56lb. "We had boiled pike and roast pike till we were tired of it." Doubting the tale at first, I was referred to two more companions living in the neighbourhood, who were with him at the time. I believe the man, though others may not.

A Pike of Unusual Size

'Straw Hat', *The Fishing Gazette* (25th February, 1899)

'A pike of unusual size', says 'Straw Hat', has been observed in the Avon, near Evesham. The monster may be occasionally seen sailing along to Charlton weir-pool. Several have had a try for him. One man went for him with an anchor, baited with a dead sheep; but he broke one of the flukes, and sailed off again. Another tried with a boat-hook (dry fly fishing) with his wife's new hat, trimmed with scarlet geraniums; but nearly lost his life in swimming back.

The habitat of this giant is in the narrow part of the river (40 yards wide), and such is the size of the pike, that he has to go to Charlton weir-pool, where the river widens out, before he can find space to turn round. He tried a somersault the other day to get round, and fell across stream, blocking the channel until he got back into the river again. I'll have this little beauty on my roach pole.

The Loch Tummel Monster

James Macnee, *The Fishing Gazette* (27th October, 1894)

Seven years ago I saw and measured the skeleton of a pike found by Mr Stewart on the bank of a small pond, connected with Loch Tummel. Without the head, the bone measured 5 feet 10 inches in length. The remains were taken to London by an English gentleman, and examined by the late Frank Buckland, Esq. The largest pike caught in Loch Tummel was captured, I believe, by myself, 28lb. This season I got one close on 24lb; but I believe that monsters do exist, though never caught, the reason being, in my opinion, that the mere mouthful - toothful, I ought to say - of a lure used, won't tempt them.

Thus James Macnee of Loch Side, Pitlochry, wrote to *The Fishing Gazette* in 1894. James Macnee had made up some flies for R.B. Marston, the editor, with this difference - the wings were made from pike scales and were used successfully by him and his friends, so much so that the editor advised, 'Where fish are shy, the hare's ear, blue and yellow duns, and quilled gnats (red, green and grey), all dressed small on fine drawn gut, with pike scale wings, should be used.'

The 109lb Tinkers' Pike

Edward Earle, *The Fishing Gazette*

Sir, - Mr Francis's paper and the many letters and paragraphs touching the size and weight of *Esox lucius* have not escaped my notice. Although I have been fortunate enough in the old country and elsewhere to kill some very heavy fish - 42 1/2 lb, 36 1/2 lb, 33 1/2 lb and 33lb respectively [meaning salmon], the first and last with fly and single gut - I never succeeded in taking a leviathan pike, nor could I ever get a record beyond 15lb in weight. I used to be disappointed at the time, for I often fished in good, large-fish holding waters.

Turning over recently some of my angling notebooks of auld lang syne, looking up a record of those days, I came across the two paragraphs [opposite], clipped from the 'Fishing' columns of the *Perthshire*

Journal and Constitutional, of which my friend - in those days - Mr J. Watson Lyall was editor. I wonder if he is still alive, and if he has added to his large stock of amusing stories. Should he still be above terra firma and this should meet his eye, I will *en passant* tell him that all Greenland's icy mountains and India's coral strand have not succeeded in erasing the pleasant memories of a cold May morning's drive from Perth to Loch Leven, when he recounted and kept one roaring by describing an incident in a laird's household, and how it happened that "The plates's all brucken and I am awa."

But *revenons à nos moutons*: I have digressed, and I own up. The monster pike below I must leave to Mr Francis and others of that ilk to ferret out - if so be their pleasure - and reduce to creditable size for its present mammoth weight spicily suggests Munchausen ancestry.

The other paragraph appears misheaded, and methinks 'A lucky par' would be more in keeping and to the point than 'A voracious pike'. A par is a fragile beastie; the teeth of *lucius* are unfriendly and sharp, his digestion powerful and rapid. Your readers will sum up the probabilities, draw conclusions, and doubtless receive the clipping with caution.

A Voracious Pike

A few days ago when the Douchfour salmon fishers were engaged at their vocation, a pike weighing about 1 1/2lb was caught in this cut, and on being opened a live fry was found in its stomach. The future salmon was at once dropped into the water, and made its exit with great celerity, evidently pleased with its escape from the prison in which it had temporarily been confined.

P.J. and C. (6th June, 1867)

Huge Pike. - A pike of extraordinary size is reported to have been lately caught at Lough . . . (the name of the water has been rubbed out, but was probably Lough Derg). The fish was caught by two tinkers, who went from Limerick to fish the lough. The enormous fish weighed 109lb.

P. J. and C. (4th July, 1867, Jamaica W.I.)

The Big Drain Pike that Couldn't Turn Round

J.H.P. (Castlebar) *The Fishing Gazette* (24th June, 1899)

I see a remark in *The Field* as to the largest pike caught by line or net. I remember seeing a pike at least 5 feet long. I don't know the weight, but it must have been between 40lb and 56lb. It was taken in a drain off the Shannon, and was so long it could not turn round. Although the drain was 6 feet wide it got into shallow water, and the sides shelving down towards the bottom prevented it from turning. It was bought by a priest in Carrick-on-Shannon; and there is a man now alive in Carrick that saw it - Mr John Burn, butcher - and I suppose many others. I mention his name, as the priest is dead. It was a bad fish. I think the men who caught it were tenants of Mr Wynne Peyton, of Springfield, near Carrick, and that Lieut. Col. John Peyton, 7th Dragoon Guards, was his eldest son. I remember the circumstance well; two men carried it on a pole through the gills. They were 5 feet 8 inches or 9 inches certainly, and though carried on their shoulders the tail was on the ground at least 9 inches. Another circumstance I can tell you as to a larger pike. There is a gentleman at present living in Douglas, Isle of Man - whose name I need not mention, but who can be referred to if you wish - who assured me he saw a pike in Buncomb Lake, near Erne, within two miles of Ballyheow, near Castlebar, and he was so large he really frightened him, and made him drive the boat he was in to shore and jump out of her. He pledges his word he was at least 6 feet long, and had an immense body. He said he never got such a fright in his life, and he did not venture on the lake again for some time. If he had a man with him he would have endeavoured to shoot him or spear him, but he only had a little boy. There are also very large pike in Lough Conn, near Ballina, at Pontoon.

A Monster Pike

John Knechtly, *The Fishing Gazette* (15th June, 1877)

It may interest some of your readers that on the 22nd May last a monster pike of 60 Kilos (about 130lb English) was caught by net in the lake of Constance by two fishermen named Adlermeister and Obermann. The fish was bought for 100 francs by Mr Steuermeister, of the Wienorhof Hotel, at Hard, and when cut open a full grown wild duck was found inside. My information is from the daily *St. Gall* paper of May 26.

Rev. William Henry's Pike

In the first edition of *Mammoth Pike* I could only record (from a reference in *The Field* of 1896) the barest details of this pike. Its captor was unknown to me as was the method of its capture.

In April 1980 I found the original allusion to the pike published in *The Field,* 11th March, 1876, the year when the pike was caught. The piece bore the title 'Capture of a Big Pike'.

I caught a pike, weighing 37¾ lb, yesterday in Lough Ramor, under rather curious circumstances. I had a small net, about 8 yards long, set in shallow water, in order to catch perch for set hooks. As I approached the net I perceived on the other side of it something sticking up out of the water, which I thought was the top of a log; I soon, however, saw that it moved about, and I at once guessed that it was the fin of a large pike. I cautiously moved in the boat round the net, and got pretty close up to the fish. He did not seem the least frightened, and merely moved languidly a few inches. While I was thinking how I could properly manage to secure him, having neither gaff, landing net, spur, nor anything of the kind, he made a brisk attempt to run out into the lake, passing between me and the net. To prevent this, I ran out my oar and headed him, on which he (still in a careless, indifferent way) ran against the net, recoiled, ran against it again, and very leisurely and composedly rolled himself up in it. Not till then did he seem aware of his danger; then he tore and flung, and splashed and dashed about, but he was too late. He had torn the net to pieces, but he had welded it so tightly and satisfactorily round him that he could not escape, and I was enabled to grasp him behind the head, and lug him, net and all, into the boat. Had he at first driven with his full force against the net, he would have gone through it, like a bullet through glass; but his tactics were marked by a special amiability for which I cannot feel too grateful. He was a very peculiar shaped fish. I never saw a pike like him before. He was only $51^1/_2$ inches long - much shorter than one of 28lb, which we took last year - but he was enormously thick, measuring 25 inches round his shoulder. His head was not long and tapering, but very broad. The depth of the water where I first saw him was about $2^1/_2$ feet. He was in splendid condition and enormously fat.

Only some two months before, *The Field* had published another letter from another Reverend gentleman Denis Knox writing from the same address namely, Virginia Rectory, Cavan. It would seem that these two Reverend gentlemen accounted for a brace of pike whose aggregate weight must have exceeded 100lb!

Instance of Voracity in the Pike

Denis Knox, Virgina Rectory, Co. Cavan (15th January)

I caught a pike yesterday measuring a trifle under 2 foot 6 inches long. I perceived the tail of another in his mouth, and, drawing it carefully out, I found, to my amazement, that in length it was only 5 inches shorter than the one that had swallowed it. It was, however, a very narrow fish, which rendered its deglutition comparatively easy. The lake here (Lough Ramor) produces very large pike. I caught one weighing 28lb, on a set hook, two years ago. The line was by no means a strong one, and had I come at it when first hooked, it would no doubt have escaped; but it had quite wearied itself out, and was dead beat when I arrived on the scene of action. I lost one which must have been a veritable monster, last summer. The set hook was bedded on new and extremely strong whipcord; the fish broke this, and got off. About three weeks afterwards a respectable farmer, who lives on the other side of the lake, told me he had found (about a week before he saw me) an immense pike, dead and nearly putrid, on the shore, with a hook in his jaw and cord attached. He measured it, and it was 5 feet long. This, I feel certain, must have been the fellow that got away from me.

The Mannheim Pike

John Hewitson *The Fishing Gazette*

The following extraordinary tales of the pike extracted from the *Saturday Magazine*, October 22nd, 1836, may be interesting to readers of your valuable paper.

In 1497, a pike was taken at Kaiserslautern in the palatinate of the Rhine, which weighed 350lb; a painting of this fish is now in the Castle of Lauterne, and the skeleton was preserved at Mannheim. The Emperor Barbarossa had placed this fish in the lake in the year 1250, with a ring of gilded copper attached to it, so constructed as to be able to expand with the growth of the fish, so that when taken, a period of 247 years had elapsed from the period when it had been reconsigned to the lake encumbered with this singular memento.

Pike Fishing in Ireland

The Fishing Gazette *(28th February, 1891)*

Before parting with the attractive subject of fishing in the free waters in the west of Ireland, I wish to tell the pike fisher that he will find rare sport with this fish in most of the lakes and in many of the rivers in Mayo, where it attains a great size. The upper waters of the Shannon, near Banagher and Meelick, also abound with enormous pike, which have been caught as heavy as 50lb.

This is a great weight, but you will be told that there are even heavier pike in that river. When I was in its vicinity last year, I heard of one which must be - if half the stories told of him be true - the grand, or rather great grandsire of Irish pike; in fact, the patriarch of the *Esox lucius* tribe. His favourite haunt - for I am informed that he has not yet been captured - is a deep, large pool, below the Queen's Salmon Gap at Meelick. There he levies blackmail on the shoals of salmon fry as they endeavour to pass through the gap, besides indulging in occasional trout and other fish.

During many seasons, almost every angler who visited Meelick has tried to catch this huge water monster, always, however, with the same result - loss of tackle. Numberless have been the encounters; but, like a giant guarding an enchanted pass, the 'great pike of the gap' sent back all his assailants shorn of their tackle and honours.

For he was no craven, but stoutly met each new foe, adding continually to the list of his triumphs. The spoils of these must be rather uncomfortable decorations, if there be any foundation for the assertion solemnly made and corroborated in the most impressive manner by a discomfited angler, who declared that 'if anyone took that pike he might set up a fishing-tackle shop with all the hooks and gimp adorning his jaws.'

The same angler stated that on one occasion when he had hooked this pike he saw his vast proportions, for he had contrived to get him alongside of the boat from which he was fishing. Being asked why he had not gaffed him, he replied:

"Oh, 'tis easy to say 'gaff him', but when I desired my attendant to perform that operation the fellow funked, and swore that the pike would upset the boat, and in the meantime the brute dived down like lightning, and carried away my tackle."

This angler and a brother officer actually journeyed to Dublin for the sole purpose of procuring tackle of extraordinary strength and peculiar construction to capture the 'pike of the gap'.

A relation of mine, a skilful and experienced angler, was tempted to try his luck with the big fish. Accordingly he constructed a trolling apparatus such as is not to be seen every day. It consisted of three large Limerick hooks, but as they were not large enough, my relation had two more constructed, under his own superintendence, by an intelligent country smith. On these five hooks, tied on the strongest gimp, he mounted as bait a trout above two pounds weight, and attached the whole to a stout hemp line wound on a large wooden reel, the concern being far too heavy to be managed by a rod. Thus equipped, he went forth strong in the belief that he was destined to kill the monster pike. Directing his boatman to row slowly backward and forward across the pool, he kept moving his hand, feeling gently as he trolled the line. Suddenly he felt a violent jerk, which, from its unyielding nature, he conjectured was occasioned by striking rocks, of which the pool was by no means free. However, the shock was but momentary, and he drew in his line to see if all was right, when he found, with feelings which a brother angler may realise, that his bait was gashed across in four or five places quite to the bone - in fact, regularly 'crimped' - and one of the large hooks was broken off at the bend.

Irish waters seem indeed to be particularly congenial to the propagation and growth of pike. The fine and picturesque lake in Lord Rosse's demesne is full of these fish, which, although they have large shoals of roach and dace to feed upon, lose no opportunity of indulging in a plethoric meal on a brother in distress. (Indeed, one captured a short time before I visited Parsonstown weighed 57lb; two others, 47lb and 43lb respectively.)

With the view of obtaining some roach and dace for bait, drum-nets were set over-night in the lake here referred to; on taking them up in the morning, from two to six enormous pike were found in each net, with about half-a-dozen other pike averaging 3lb each, all more or less mangled by the large pike which had entered the nets to prey on their small kindred, which had in the first instance been doubtless attracted to the nets by the roach which they had devoured.

Each attempt to catch small fish for bait resulted in the capture of pike, which, however, were so large and powerful as to speedily reduce the drum-nets to a condition of inefficiency. The notorious sporting voracity of Master Jack at certain seasons and certain days, when '*Das Wasser rauscht, das Wasser school*', should lead you to regard him as worthy of being artistically fished for.

On such days at least as he is on the feed eschew base baits, and substitute that wondrous lure known by the name of the pike fly, to which the gaudiest and most extraordinary salmon fly is tame and colourless in comparison.

With such a fly, scarlet bodied, two big bright heads for eyes, wings of flaunting peacock's feathers, and carrying at its tail sauce piquant, in the shape of enormous hooks, you will, on auspicious days and in good pike water, have rare sport.

I have felt the rush of a large and strong salmon, and declare that that of a twenty-pound pike when he has seized a fly and discovered his mistake is nearly, if not quite, as exciting. I was fishing one day from a small skiff in the lake on Lord Rosse's estate with a pike fly of enormous size, the day being very rough and the waters high; when just as I had worked the fly up close to the boat, and was making ready to cast it again, I beheld a vast pair of green-hued cavernous jaws issuing from the water near the boat close to the fly, and with a rush that made the big salmon wheel scream, away went the great fish to the water depths, carrying out without a check fifty yards of line. Nor did he stop then, for, having no more line to give him, he actually commenced towing my little skiff, which was just large enough for one person; and so strong was the fish that I was quite unable, for upwards of half an hour, to recover a yard of line, and when at length I succeeded in bringing him to a pause, he repeatedly manifested his disinclination to make my acquaintance by tremendous rushes, comparable only to those made by a large fish-run salmon or white trout when they carry out all the line. It was well that this and my rod were very strong, otherwise the pike would soon have effected a divorce with the tempting fly; but as it was I had no apprehension of a rupture of the tackle as long as I could keep clear of weeds near the shore. This, however was difficult; for when the pike took a fancy to make a rush I was obliged to hold the rod with both my hands, which were thus unable to control the boat by the use of the oars. It was only when my captive remained quiet that I was at all able to manage the boat, an operation rendered additionally difficult by the high wind which was blowing. In this manner upwards of an hour passed, and I began to despair of getting my pike. My only chance was in landing in a locality free from weeds; but even then I knew that I could not kill the pike unassisted. At length I saw a labourer approaching the lake, and by shouting made him hear that I wanted a gaff. While he was absent procuring this, I succeeded in rowing the boat close to a favourable part of the shore, retaining the butt end of the rod between my knees, and allowing the line to run out so as not to disturb the pike, which had gone to the bottom. On the arrival of the man with the gaff I leaped on shore, and now, having solid ground under me, and great faith in the strength of my tackle, I commenced a new series of operations, which terminated by the pike becoming my prize about two hours after I had hooked him. He weighed 27lb, and was in admirable condition.

The Lost Monster

Richard Walker

In August 1967, on this particular day, we had a rough passage from Balmaha to Portnellan. The waves were breaking and quite a lot of spindrift was blowing about. Fred Buller and Pete Thomas shared one boat, Ken Taylor and I the other. As the only member of the party with no claim to be a 'former naval person', I was relieved to reach the calmer water between the islands and the shore at Portnellan, and also to find myself within casting distance of the very spot where, in 1947, Tom Morgan had caught his huge 47lb 11oz pike.

A channel runs between the small islands and the shore of the loch in this area, a route for sea-trout and salmon on the way to the River Endrick, and between this channel and the shore there is a long strip of dense wiry potamogeton weed. Some of this weed also forms a big bed next to the largest of the small islands. Buller and Thomas anchored their boat with killicks at the edge of this latter weed-bed; Ken and I fetched up moored across the channel, with our boat end-on to the other and about thirty yards from it, so that we had weed not far away at bow and stern; a small island, only a few yards across, about fifty yards ahead as we faced east; and beyond the other boat, a long narrow island, covered like the small one with scrub willows, about seventy yards from us and forty yards from Fred and Pete. Far beyond this narrow island we could see the purple-blue peaks of Ben Lomond and the other mountains; in the other direction, the grassy shore of the loch, with grazing cattle, rose quite steeply. Some oyster-catchers were prospecting along the beach, and beyond the small island, a family of mergansers were finding something interesting among the weeds. With the sun shining and only a few fleecy clouds in the sky, it was a very pleasant scene.

What was to happen concerns only Fred Buller, so I need not describe the tackle and methods that the rest of us were using. Fred had a powerful 10 foot 2-piece fibreglass rod with a long cork handle, and an old but thoroughly sound Allcock Aerial reel, $4^1/_2$ inches in diameter, carrying about 200 yards of 23lb b.s. braided nylon line. This was knotted to a stranded wire trace of about 30lb b.s., to which I had whipped securely, with silk and copper wire, a No. 4 taper-shank treble hook. Our usual pike tackles carry two trebles but Fred, for some reason, chose on this occasion the single-treble tackle, with a sliding celluloid cigar-shaped float on the line.

He baited his hook with a dead roach, quite a large one weighing about 3/4 lb, and gently swung it out so that it sank on to a hard bottom in about six feet of very clear water, only six yards from the boat. There it lay for only a few minutes.

Its disappearance was the signal for the rest of us to gently raise the mooring weights and bring in our own deadbaits (our prearranged plan to avoid the hazard of getting fouled-up). But the pike which caused this activity proved to be very small, indeed the smallest pike (so Buller said) he had ever taken from that bay even though he had fished it with live-baits for over fourteen years.

The tackle was rebaited with what looked like an even bigger dead-bait and dropped on to the same spot; within a minute and before the rest of us had had time to get our own dead-baits into position Thomas was drawing Buller's attention to yet another run. The latter tightened on the pike almost immediately - he having listened to and responded to my own pet dictum on when to strike a big pike:

"If that's the pike you've come all this way for - you don't need to wait before striking; it will have a mouth like a coal bucket - if it isn't the one you want and your strike is a bit previous, it won't matter if you miss it - will it?"

In descriptions of hooking big fish, it is common to read that at this stage 'it felt as if I'd hooked the bottom'. I don't know whether that is how it felt to Fred, but that is exactly how it looked to me, for his rod took on a considerable bend without whatever was at the end of his line moving an inch. It stayed so for what seemed minutes but was probably no more than twenty seconds; then a vast swirl appeared on the surface, so big that in that moment I realised that Fred was into a fish of quite exceptional size. I could see and hear Pete Thomas getting his tackle out of the way and then, as the fish moved towards their boat, preparing to pull up the mooring weights.

Up to this time the hooked fish had done nothing spectacular; it simply resisted the pull from Buller for a time; then, coming towards the boat, it must have seen the anglers in it, for it sheered round and made off, coming towards the boat in which Ken and I sat and evidently making for the large, dense weedbed beyond us.

As it neared us, Fred increased the pressure on the

fish, which was not moving at any great speed, and this had the effect of bringing it to the surface, which happened when it was no more than six or seven feet from the side of our boat, near the stern where I was fishing. Had I had the 5 foot gaff in my hand I could have reached out and gaffed it easily, and if I'd known what was to follow, I might have done exactly that.

I didn't know. I sat amazed at the sight of what was by far the biggest fish of any kind that I have ever seen in fresh water. I am not without experience of big fish, having seen both carp and salmon of over 40lb both in the water and on the bank, as well as several pike well over 30lb. This fish was in a class above any of those. It looked as if it could eat a 20-pounder, and I was seeing it in very clear water, in bright light and at close range. I shall never forget it as long as I live. It was moving quite slowly but with tremendous power. I guessed it as measuring about 5 feet in length and some 10 inches across the back.

It forged on past our boat; then Fred's rod straightened and he gave an exclamation of disappointment; the fish was off. A disturbance in the weeds subsided and that was the end. When he wound up his line, Fred found that the knot to the trace had given way and proceeded to blame himself for having failed to tie it more carefully and to test it for strength.

Later, he asked Ken and me what we thought the fish weighed. After explaining that neither of us had previous experience of fish of that size, we said it must have been more than 50lb; on that we were emphatically agreed. That is what we said at the time; I now confess that for my own part, the estimate I gave Fred was conservative, to reduce his disappointment. I thought then and think now that the fish was bigger than that.

Many years later, I worked out a formula for calculating the weight of pike and other fish of similar shape from length and girth measurements, which has proved remarkably accurate. If my guess about the length and breadth of back of Fred's lost fish was accurate, the formula supplies a weight of about 65lb.

Many years later, in 1986, Brian Clarke recounted in the *Sunday Times Magazine* the story of how he had found the dead body of this huge Portnellan pike. In response to this he received the following letter from Charles Docherty:

Dear Mr Clarke

I have just read your article on Mr Fred Buller about the pike which he lost.

It may just be coincidence but back in 1967 I was walking on the shores of Loch Lomond, just below Balmaha, towards the mouth of the River Endrick, where I came across the partial remains of a monster pike.

The fish had drowned.

The fish had been securely hooked in the scissors but the wire trace with swivel was wrapped around the snout preventing the fish from breathing.

It was clearly a very large fish, although the birds etc. had reduced its size considerably.

I recovered the wire trace, but unfortunately it has disappeared with the passage of time.

Perhaps you would be good enough to let Mr Buller have this information, which might throw some light on the one that got away!

Yours sincerely
Charles M. Docherty

A Day on Lake and River

Edward F. Spence K.C. from The Pike Fisher *(1928)*

A day on the Hampshire Avon, a lovely river whereon I have striven as angler at many places; near Downton, in Lord Nelson's water - spinning only allowed; in three waters at or by Downton. At and below Breamore, at Fordingbridge, Ringwood and a long stretch below; Winkton, and at Christchurch in the Royalty Fishery and the Hotel waters. And in the splendid stream I have caught sea-trout, trout, grayling, pike, perch, tench, chub, roach, dace, gudgeon, minnows, eels and white bream; also bass, grey mullet and flounders, and I have loved - and lost - one of its many salmon, which broke my hook intended for 'chavender or chub' opposite to the slaughter-house of Mr Reeks.

This time Downton was the venue and the holiday, Christmas. Indeed, it was on Christmas Day itself that we set out for the river, a longish tramp through the picturesque village and across fields and water meadows. Heavily laden, since we three were carrying lunch and a bottle of Burgundy, rods and tackle for pike fishing and bait catching, cloaks, wraps, camera and a bait-can, a rather light bait-can, for the boatman had told someone else to take it overnight with its two dozen dace to the river, and the someone else had told someone else, wherefore we found it next morning in the stable yard with twenty corpses in it and the four survivors of this Calcutta business, looking pale at the gills.

When crossing one of the water meadows the man and I stopped to refill the can and relight our pipes whilst the third of the party went forward. In the distance a little crowd of men. "Poaching a drain," said the boatman to me, and then we heard the voice of the guileless companion. "Will you kindly stand a moment? I want to take a photograph."

And they folded their (nets) like the Arabs,
And as silently stole away.

This with apologies to Longfellow for a trifling alteration.

When we reached the boat-house Frank, the man, hurried to the big, wooden live-bait box lying in the stream, for there were hopes of bait in it. "Dang it," said he, "someone has forced lock," and all we found was a big roach, six ounces or so, half covered with a kind of green moss, but lively, so we put it into the well. 'Let well alone', the English version of Voltaire's '*Le mieux est l'ennemi du bien*', is a wise maxim for little fish.

Off we went slowly down stream, simply letting live-baits swim ahead and checking them at each little drain or draw leading water from the meadows. "Won't get much," observed Frank, "till hoar frost melts." Sadly true. By the time we reached the islands the sun was hot, and the grass green, whilst a sou'-west breeze blew sweetly. What a spot the big eddy between the two islands used to be, slowly revolving, irregularly, and on each side a swift rush of the river. "Queer," said Frank after a while, "wind all right, water nice colour, frost melted - always gets a run here." This time was the unhappy exception. So we moved out after changing the bait, for the common fate had overtaken them, and as we started a pike came up and grabbed one of the dead dace thrown upon the water. "*Farceur, va,*" said my companion, and Frank made a more energetic remark.

As we struck the stream the wind went right round with a rush to the north-east. "Dang it, that's bad!" but even as he spoke a float went down and a few minutes later my companion landed a three-pound fish! And fifty yards lower one of the same size came at my float.

"Now we'd better go to the bridge and catch bait."

"Put on big roach, and let the lady try 'longside right bank above bridge. I see a big fish feed there th' other marnin'."

Yard after yard - lovely water twelve feet deep and slow on the edge of the stream near the bank, tiny eddies at the ends of the drains. I walked behind the boat, spinning. Suddenly a little scream. I looked up; twenty yards below the boat the big roach, although set at nine feet, was swimming on the surface in mad circles and then 'Crash, splash!' and a big fish had jumped half out of the water to grab it. So throwing down my rod I rushed to the boat and jumped in. The pike was tearing across the river dragging the rod down.

"Hold up the point, my dear."

"*Mais mon ami c'est si fort - Ohé quel beau poisson!*" But she got it up stoutly.

"Her have struck un fine," said Frank, "good fish near twenty I allow."

"*Plus que ça, mon ami!* But if I lose it. *Quel poisson!*" No wonder that she was excited, never before having caught anything above seven pounds. It was getting unpleasantly close to the rushes on the left bank, and

Frank was dropping the boat below the fish.

"Now you must reel in hard," said I, "or shall I help?"

"*Mais non, mais non, mon ami!* I'll catch it alone myself or lose it; but if I do, *quel malheur.*" Setting her teeth she ground at the reel and the pike's head came round. Time after time it put out that head and shook fiercely and then came a quiet, steady struggle to reach the right bank. The effort of the fish and the rush of the fast river caused a heavy strain on the unaccustomed wrists of the lady; but she stuck bravely to her task and the boatman aided her by working to the quieter water on the right bank where there was no danger point.

"*Oh le brochet est fatigué, vite avec le filet.*"

I got out the big net - "length of the rod length of the line, my dear and pull it back"; then the net did its fell work and bang came the pike into the boat almost on top of our dog, Mops, who barked without ceasing, almost bursting with excitement during the whole episode.

"Fine fish mum, and well handled; about seventeen pound."

"Not twenty?"

"No mum, not quite, scale won't show more; but lovely condition, and wot a fighter!"

"Yes, my dear," I said, answering a question that was

not asked. "Kill it, Frank and I'll have it set up."

"*Oui, mon ami*, a very little drop and much water," so we all three drank the health of the corpse and Mopseman, so named after the Rat-wife's dog in 'Little Eyolf', was allowed to lick the nose of his mistress's victim. Alas, poor Mops, prettiest and cleverest of mongrels and keenly interested in fishing during a long, merry life now ended. The pike was sixteen and a half pounds.

Then we had to drop down to the railway bridge, below the arches of which near the left bank plenty of roach were always to be seen, but not always to be caught. An awkward place with a very irregular bottom. This time the fish were provoking; contemptible 'tiddlers' grabbed in a hurry, hoary fathers of the flock far too big for bait, pulled down the float with majestic motion but the two to four ounces were coy. At last we had caught half a dozen and so went down to the water near the Agricultural College there to try for bait and also pike. No great catch of either, and I got out of the boat to spin and had the pleasure of seeing Madame run five pike and land four, each of about five pounds.

A little later we drifted to the weir pool and with paternosters each got a pike in an eddy - neither over four pounds.

Then a tragedy. A pike took her bait and dashed off into the foaming water so fiercely that she could not hold it back. "A big 'un!" shouted Frank, "I see 'un curl." Here and there in short rushes but invisible always. "Drag it up, my dear! Risk it." "Oh, *mon Dieu!* It's gone slack - no it's tight, but I can't move it. *Quel chameau!*"

Clearly the line or trace was round or under something. We pulled this way and that - and went to the opposite side of the weir to get a different angle. No good. "Give a lot of slack, it may free itself." And by some sort of Houdini performance it did, and the fish dashed off merrily.

"*Quel le chance, c'est plus grand que l'autre - quel dommage de l'avoir tué.*" But alas, another dead stop, and this time after all sorts of pulling and humouring the line came back broken above the trace. "I'm glad," she said sorrowfully, "it's only got a single hook in its mouth, *mais quel cochon*! We won't fish here any more."

So back to the main stream; several runs, and one pike of six pounds - to my rod. Then a farce. A big tug at my float, a pike that ran thirty yards at the least down stream and rushing back dived deep into the weeds. It seemed a good fish. "Don't you beat mine," said my companion, "and I hope you will, and if it's over twenty pounds I'll sell my sables - not you my dear little Mops - to pay for the stuffing." Frank got up the anchor and we drifted down. Leaning over the boat I grasped the line, pulled hard and up came a fish of barely five pounds! Foul-hooked.

"One more try," said the lady.

"We're below the water, mum," answered Frank.

"That's all right," and she dropped in her bait and down the float went within six feet of the boat. A good stiff fight, with hopes and fears and wild guesses and a complication caused by Mops falling overboard - his feet were always on the gunwale if a fish was being played; he knew all about angling. At last a nine pounder came in, was unhooked, was licked by Mops and returned. Then a stiff pull and a long walk and back to the Bull Inn, tired, happy, hungry; and we had a leg of four-year-old mutton such as you do not get nowadays - *Hélas*!

A Day on the Lake

"A bit of a frost in the night," said the boatman - the term 'gillie' is not used on the lake - Slapton Ley! "Water looks a bit clearer down along."

"Shan't do much till the day's warm. Look at the nice green paint." The nice green paint was the vivid green scum at the edge of the water which during that summer and autumn was infested by a cruel kind of algae affecting the sport badly, for it rendered the water so thick and highly coloured that the pike could not see the bait at distance, and the rudd had little of the brilliance which they should be showing in October. Lots of weed about and the one cheering fact that the water was very low so that the pike were collected in a much smaller area than usual - a sort of 'Congested Area' but not in Ireland.

Off we row through thickly weeded water noticing the wake of two or three pike disturbed by the boat. Vain casts here and there into holes in the weed with a rudd on a wobbly tackle - a favourite bait; the small perch was not showy enough. Near the north-west bank opposite to the landing stage was a clear stretch of water about two hundred yards long and forty in width. Three casts and then a fourth: a grab, a strike, and a pike was rushing for the weeds but had to come back, another rush or two but it was only a little 'un - four pounds - and was forced to come into the boat for operations with the disgorger after which it sailed off gladly. One more run in the clear space, this time a sturdy six-pounder which managed to get right down into the weed of a deepish hole near the old stone gate-post and required some hand-lining.

After this a long, long blank. All round the bay careful spinning found nobody 'at home' either close to the rushes or in the middle, but lots of bits of weed to be picked or shaken off.

From the bay we went to the main water, paid useless calls at the 'Parlour' - 'Two Trees' and then 'Three Trees,' all famous places. A boat was anchored by the rushes near 'Cow Point' with live-baiters in it: a hundred yards short of them I got a run at my sprat, for I had changed bait and was trying sprat on an Abbey Mills - a good hard run by a stout fish which kept out of sight during five minutes of stern struggle and then, alas, got off.

The live-baiters in answer to polite enquiries said that five pike had run and three fish were landed, one of them reaching nine pounds and also that the bait were biting well.

After spinning fruitlessly round the shore above 'Cow Point' we decided to try 'the Gulf' where I once had seventy-six pounds of pike live-baiting after tea during a thunderstorm; very weedy by the west bank where the rushes are thick but a long clear spot on the shore which shelves quite swiftly to deep water. Not a touch near the rushes. On the shore close to the edge two ladies were basking in the sun which was shining delightfully. My bait fell so close as to startle them. A yard or two of spin and then plonk; a pike leaped half out of the water and seized the bait. "Ooo," shrilled one of the ladies. The fish seemed anxious to show off before them and played fiercely; ran off twenty yards of line the reel screaming - darted back under the boat, got head out of water to shake it, dived deep into weed and was hand lined up. Great admiration from the bank, the ladies coming down to the edge and shouting this and that. At last the quarry was tired out, so into the net a seven pounder; hooks out quickly, then the spring balance and back to the lake. "Oh," called one spectator to the other, "they've thrown it back; how silly," and the answer, loud enough, intentionally, for me - "I wish he'd given it to me." A quarter of an hour more in the Gulf vainly, and as we rowed off I heard, "I don't believe he knows how to fish - there must be lots more - look how quickly he caught that one!" Are the lady pike more logical?

After pulling, punting and shoving through a cutting in the reeds we came to 'Eel Trunk', so called because there used to be a trap or trunk for eels: a trench with a drop door. It was supposed that the simple-minded creatures, believing that it led to the sea, would swim up it in the hope of getting into the abyssal waters off Sicily, there to celebrate the marriage, after which they die. For the eel loves but once in its life and can honestly sing of himself like the slave in Heine's pretty poem:

And my race is of those Asras,
Who, when'er they love must perish.

Quite heroes of romance the eels whether they are 'snig', 'grig' or the flat-nosed - if they be different species - but not such fools as to go up that trench. Queer place 'Eel Trunk'; for years it was the most likely spot in the lake to get a run, indeed almost a place of certainty. At one time we - 'Long John' Pepperell and I - used to leave it unspun when going down the lake as a kind of reserve in case we did badly 'down along'. Of late years a blank is the certainty. Why? There are no discernible changes of shore, water, rushes or reeds to explain its desertion by the pike, and plenty of rudd and perch still haunt it. A like phenomenon is noticeable in the case of two or three other 'shops' on this water.

We fixed up close to the reeds fifty yards above 'Eel Trunk' and out went two baits, one on float tackle straight across the gentle breeze, and the other on a float paternoster alongside of the reeds, and then rods and lines were prepared for the important job of catching more bait.

"Have you got 'em?" I asked.

"Yes, sir," replied the boatman, a veteran who had been through the battle of Jutland and never spoke of it unasked: he produced a bit of newspaper wrapped up in which were bright red berries. We had been experimenting with elderberries, blackberries, dried currants and small sultanas and the rudd and perch had taken them very well if not quite as well as the worms and the gentles - though I come from the North I do not call them 'maggots' or 'maggits' nowadays. The dullness of their hue in the dark water was somewhat against them.

The new bait was the asparagus berry, not, indeed, of the famous *Asperge d'Argenteuil* but good English stuff. A lot of perch and rudd, mostly too big for our purpose, took the pretty berries. What a number of baits for coarse fish there are which the books do not mention, the 'chavender or chub' being the only quarry regarded as almost omnivorous. The perch - I have caught him with all the baits mentioned above, and with little live fish, and bits of dead fish simply stuck on the hook, and small pieces of meat, and 'Zulu' flies and imitation shrimps (and real ones I am sure would take) and all kinds of spinning baits, natural and artificial and several sorts of grub or larva, and of course, paste and baby frogs and bread crust. No doubt some baits are better than others, but the angler should never be at a loss: let him at a pinch try anything malleable and of reasonable size.

Our live-baits did nothing. But the sun shone; the sky was blue; the small fish were biting; the waves murmured on the beach; the gulls sometimes were screaming and sometimes making their sad sound like the weeping of little children; the coot uttered low comedy noises; the swans were dashing about now with the music of 'harps in the air' from their wings and now with crashes on the water in sham chases of one another; the moorhens skittered along silently always seeming to be in a desperate hurry; at times a dusky cormorant - a sea crow his name says, but we called him a 'shag' - was visible flying quickly past: I have never seen a shag sitting on a tree like Satan but, apparently Milton did. Herons lazily loafed over the water with deceptive speed; two or three rabbits were gambolling furtively on the bank; we had plenty of tobacco; lunch and beer were at hand in the hotel and so we endured the coyness of the pike patiently for an hour. And then home with only three pike to our credit weighing seventeen pounds the lot.

Of the early afternoon nothing to be said save that we 'bunged' off 'Two Trees' and then 'Three Trees' and got nothing until I had brought in one rod intending to give up that game and spin. "A run, sir," said the boatman. The big float on the other line was down but before I could pick up the rod it had reappeared. "Dropped it," he murmured, but as he spoke it disappeared again, yet the pilot was motionless. Up again, down again, up again, down again. "A baby," I remarked, "Yes, sir, that's the way they plays." "Or an eel, though October is late." "Very like an eel, sir" - oh, Polonius - "and a big 'un was took las' week." After what seemed ages, and probably was nearly ten minutes of this jiggle-joggling, I grew almost impatient. "Here goes," and here went: the strike was answered by a tug that pulled the rod point fiercely down. "Not a tiddler; not an eel," I said. However I am not out to sing the saga of that pike, a sturdy fellow weighing close upon ten pounds.

Again we spun 'Cow Point' and the western boundary and across the middle - we might as well have spun the neighbouring sandhills. Then to the eastern boundary and we spun the lanes through the weed, strips of clear water twenty feet wide - 'be the same more or less' as we lawyers say - and only a few inches of water over weed. Four runs and three fish landed; two and a half, three and five pounds. From there north spinning along the thick reeds; and opposite to a small break in them a little pluck - nothing; another pluck - nothing - what are those queer plucks? Certainly pike make them; are they, perhaps, at the lead? Then a feeling of dead weight like the drag of weed, and but for the plucks I should not have struck. When I did there was a feeling of quiet resistance. I reeled in steadily - no struggle. Against my habit I was standing up; suddenly a pike and I saw one another at a few yards distance. Off he tore towards the reeds until I had to hold fast and give no more line risking a breakage. Not a heroic fish: it fought poorly for its twelve pounds of weight but struggled tremendously for a minute or two when in the boat. A long thin fellow badly scarred by some monster so we put it back to look for the 'Dr Tench' of romantic writers, who, however, has no address in this lake.

Then we tried the boundary: right out in the middle nearly two furlongs from shore, reed or rush but much haunted, towards evening by old hands for good reason. With complicated feelings we watched a spinner, quite a decent workman, run and land three fish whilst we had none. "A spoon," he answered to a shouted enquiry, "all about five pound." But I stuck to a rudd on a wobbling tackle.

Suddenly, 'vlan, bing, bang, boom' - those words come from a fairy tale in the Christmas number of the *Figaro Illustré*, the whole of which I once, for an unremunerative fee, translated, poetry and all except the advertisements. 'Vlan, bing, bang, boom' and the rod was almost torn from my unexpecting hands, and when the catch was on, the reel screamed like a heretic being cross-examined on the rack. "Row hard after it," I shouted; for the drum was beginning to show as clearly as the top of my poor pate. The screaming stopped. "Dropped it," moaned the boatman but I turned the handles madly till, to my joy, I found the line tight, and then out of the water came a monstrous head, as big as a pantomime giant's. "A real big 'un!" exclaimed the man, "hold 'un hard." I shoved the rod point into the water to drag down the head and so prevent the shaking out of hooks in the unresistant air. Then she came fiercely for the boat, straight for the bow doing something like even time, and I had to hold the rod down in the water almost to the reel fittings whilst I clambered to the end of the boat and passed the bending top round the stern. Off went the fish in the direction of the reeds, fortunately about a quarter of a mile off, and the men in the other boat watching us - also with complicated feelings - said that we went about three hundred yards, the boatman backing water as madly as ever a punter backed a Derby runner.

Gradually I got back the line, and at last we were a

few yards off: she lay still on the water looking much larger than she was - oh, those dear ladies and their acts of deception - and as wicked as an Army mule. The boatman put out my net, a vast affair, an optimist's net big enough for sturgeon. But no, she had got her second wind and was off again yet not for a very long run - and again for a shorter distance - and so once more, and then I took charge, pulled her hard towards the boat and over the yawning net. Crash into the boat which shivered - or was it shuddered? And lo, when the boatman stooped to seize the quarry she shook the hooks out of her mouth. "Shall I save 'un, sir?" he asked. Salvation of a fish 'down along' means a fatal blow or two on the nape of the neck. "Is it over twenty?" "Yes, sir, well over." "All right." I do not remember what was used to administer salvation: we certainly had no 'priest' on board. The spring balance said 23lb, the tape measure 42½ inches, but the London taxidermist gave twenty-two as the weight: a pound is small shrinkage in three days.

And so home, for the sun was down and pike very rarely run after that. A good day, nine pike, weight 72lb, not a great number for the lake. But how jolly for the humble angler - to the lordly salmon fisher an 'Oh, it's nothing', as Toole used to say in 'Walker, London'.

Nowadays Jane - I don't know why we called her

'Jane' but the name sticks - properly preserved and nailed to a board painted green but uncovered by glass hangs over the door of my den, politely called 'library'. And out of her cruel - glass - eyes she looks contemptuously at the masses of books, and the Blanc de Chine figures of Kwan Yin, and the Martin-ware pots and vases, and old Dutch pottery and thinks sadly, fiercely of the days when she roamed the ley fearlessly and of the fatal act of folly in taking that small wobbling rudd. Alas, poor Jane! Perhaps by way of epitaph I ought to quote three lines from a long forgotten poet, Alexander Ross:

Which her name it was Jane,
And she begged to explain,
She wouldn't do it again.

A February Pike

H. T. Sheringham, An Angler's Hours *(1905)*

So terrible was he, said one, that when he left his lair the river retreated before him, fleeing impetuously over its banks and taking refuge in the water-meadows; so ravenous was he, said another, that moor-hens and ducks shunned the spot, herons dared venture no nearer than half a mile, and even an otter had been seen in the grey of dawn hastening away with every sign of consternation in its countenance. The great pike of the previous year, said a third with conspicuous candour, weighed the better part of nineteen pounds; but even that creditable magnitude had not secured for it untroubled repose, for the unhappy fish had lived in a state of constant panic, ever dreading the time when it should be its turn to be devoured.

Only death indeed, intimated the candid one, had resolved its doubts, and that barely, for its 19lb struggles had been misinterpreted as the seduction of a wee timorous bait. The monster had come forth from the depths to take advantage of the situation, and had only been driven off by the heroism of angler and keeper, who would not submit tamely to the insolence that regarded 19lb of hard-earned pike as no better than 4oz of dace. Therefore they repelled the giant with shoutings and splashings, landed their 19-pounder, and took it away to the taxidermist; in fact, if evidence of the story were needed, the fish might now be seen in a glass case with gold letters on it.

These Gargantuan fables were, even to an intelligence enfeebled by recent influenza, obviously but the persiflage of the club, the imaginative flights that every honest angler takes from time to time into the unknown. Nevertheless, they chimed in wonderfully with the convalescent mood that suggested a holiday and a pike or so to end the season, and next day I put myself with my tackle into a cab, and then into an express train, little dreaming that I was about to enjoy the only week of spring weather that graced the year 1903, insinuated by a stroke of pleasing humour into the middle of February, where none but I could find it. When, an hour and a half afterwards, I got out at the station for which I was bound, the sun shone and the air was like wine, the wine of the South with the chill taken off. And when yet an hour later, I reached the river bank, I sat on a stile, reflected that the world is indeed good, and looked round for may-flies.

But, be the sun never so warm and an overcoat never so embarrassing, it is not given to mortal angler to see may-flies on the Kennet in February; if it were they would be vain, and a salted dace was more appropriate to the season. There was no wind, but the river was of good height and colour, so the chance of a fish or two was not so bad. It remained a chance, however, for neither by spinning nor trolling with snap-tackle was a run gained in the whole length of water at my disposal, though it must be confessed that I did not overwork myself. I was a convalescent, after all, conscience admitted, and had a perfect right to enjoy this miraculous gift of spring as I would. The keeper, who appeared with the frugal mid-day repast, was politely of the same opinion, but there was a small pike in the adjacent brook, and he would esteem it a favour if it could be removed, as it harried his trout and vexed his soul. To be brief, it was removed, and it weighed 3½ lb. This was the only fish that greeted the spring on the first day.

The second day was like unto the first, and every whit as perfect - more perfect in fact, for the keeper had procured some live baits, and the salted dace could be discarded. His mind was not, however, quite free from care, for it appeared that there was another small pike in the adjacent brook, which harried his trout and vexed his soul hardly less than the first. This also was removed with the help of a gudgeon on a paternoster, and it weighed 24¼lb; but the Kennet yielded nothing, though the keeper, cheered by slaughter, talked in somewhat Gargantuan strain of a big pike seen occasionally by himself and others. Asked if this fish had been known to cause floods, eat ducks, moorhens, and herons, alarm otters, and wrestle with anglers for a live-bait weighing 19lb, he confessed that these accounts bore the impress of exaggeration; the fish he meant would be somewhere about sixteen, and it lay just opposite the second hatch-hole in the middle field. This exactitude of detail made the fish seem a possibility, but neither spinning nor live-baiting induced him to move, and the second day ended with little done, but much enjoyed.

On the third day there was a soft vernal air after a crisp, frosty night, and I awoke to the joyful consciousness that I was fully restored to health. Sunshine had been too much even for the notorious after-effects of influenza, and there was now no reason why I should not fish as though I meant to catch something. The masters of the gentle art inform us that good intentions are not enough of themselves to bring about success; in these days of over-fishing one must also use science and fine tackle. I pondered over the matter during breakfast, and afterwards looked through my tackle-box for a trace that should satisfy the requirements of science and the remarkable weather. Eventually I picked out a rather fine Thames trout trace of single gut, soaked it, and tested it up to a dead weight of five pounds. To match it there was a flight of live-bait hooks tied on similar gut, and I observed to myself that any moderately skilful angler ought to be able to land anything with such excellent material.

Then in a state of considerable scientific elation I went off to the river, to find it the least bit ruffled by the breeze, and very suitable for the testing of my theories. I began with a live dace on float tackle, casting it out almost to the other side of the river and allowing it to swim down-stream, while I kept pace with it along the bank. And, sure enough, as it reached the spot pointed out by the keeper there was a check, the float went under, and a vigorous strike just revealed the fact that the fish was a heavy one before the trace parted at an upper knot.

Then was it borne in upon me that the sun was too hot, the breeze too mild, the season out of joint, and science a wicked delusion. Had there been a snoring breeze, had the white waves been heaving high, as even a convalescent has a right to expect when fishing for pike in February, had the still small voice of science been drowned by a conflict of the elements, I should never have thought of using a ridiculous gut trace (on which Izaak Walton himself could scarce have landed a minnow), and that 16-pounder would have been mine. Besides, I was no longer convalescent, and boisterous weather was what I needed - was no less than my due. In a word, my meditations were supremely ungrateful, and I was justly punished when the wind dropped altogether, February became more like May than ever, and not another fish moved for the rest of the day.

On the morrow, however, there was a real south-westerly wind and a fine ripple on the water. Pike, I reflected, as I mounted an 8-inch dace on a Pennell spinning-flight, have been known to run at a bait twice in a day, twice even in an hour, almost, even, twice in a minute. It was therefore logical to expect the 16-pounder that morning. Yet, by the time a third of the water had been carefully spun over without a touch, the edge of enthusiasm was to some extent blunted, and the keeper, who appeared about mid-day, was asked somewhat petulantly to explain the wrong-headedness of the fish under his charge. This, of course, he could not do, but, willing enough to tell of past triumphs, he furbished up the tale of the 19-pounder anew, and dwelt on the labour of carrying it home, accompanied as it was by two others of 14lb and 13lb respectively, both caught by the lucky fisherman on the same day.

Having done his duty by the triumphs of history he departed, and somewhat cheered I returned to my spinning, determined to give the sixteen-pounder another chance. Opposite the hatch-hole of which mention has been made, the river was deep and some thirty yards wide, but a few yards above was a shelving shallow. Spinning across and up-stream I thoroughly searched the deep water and worked up towards the shallow, making casts of about thirty-five yards. At last, in some four feet of water, I had that blessed sensation only obtained in spinning for pike, the sensation that something which suggests a stout post has come into collision with the bait, but something that sends a thrill up the line and obviously is not a post. In a second or two it became obvious that the fish was a heavy one, and I cast a hurried glance over my shoulder to see if the keeper was still in sight. He was - a microscopic figure in the distance - and I whistled with all my breath to recall him. Fortunately the sound carried, the retreating figure stopped, recognised the signal of distress, and returned at a run.

Meanwhile it was as much as I could do to play the fish and attract assistance at the same time. At first the pike moved steadily up-stream for fifty yards or so; then he came back again at a great pace, and I had to run with him, winching in line for all I was worth - a vain proceeding, as the fish immediately took it all out again. After a while, however, it became evident that the main battle was to be in the deep water, and by the time the keeper arrived proceedings had become more dignified and sedate.

"That's him," gasped the keeper, as a thick olive-green back showed for a moment close to the bank.

"Twelve pounds," I commented. "He's making a good fight for his size."

The sight of the fish suggested that it was nearly time for the net - a big grilse net - and it was not long before the gradual application of the butt told. The pike was brought in and the net was slipped under it. "He's a big twelve-pounder!" I exclaimed, when it became obvious that the net was too small, a point emphasised by the fish, which rolled out of it and hurried away to the other side of the river, fortunately still hooked. Thrice this happened, but the fourth time the quarry, utterly beaten, allowed himself to be packed inartistically into the inadequate receptacle and dragged ashore in triumph. As net and fish were carried safely out into the meadow I enlarged my estimate of him to sixteen pounds. "More," said the keeper, and it became apparent that he was right when, each holding one end of a sack, we were traversing the mile that lay between the river and a weighing-machine. By the end of the mile the more moderate estimate (the keeper's) was 40lb.

As a matter of fact, the fish weighed twenty-three pounds and a few ounces, though, as I still fondly imagine, in the glass case it looks more. The triumph was not Gargantuan, perhaps, but in such marvellous spring weather it seemed so. It is seldom that one has everything that one could desire, and that holiday was perfection. It made the influenza quite worth while.

A Tragedy of the Mere

A.J. Price, An Angler's Lines *(1911)*

My friend's float went down, and there ensued a mighty conflict betwixt fisher and fish. A gain of a few inches of line, negatived by a rush that took out more than double the quantity, a stubborn resistance to coercion, a grudging submission to the steady pressure of the rod, an apparently beaten fish, and then a dash for a jagged stake that stood up from the bed of the lake. He was round it! He was free!

Upon our lamentations there broke a sudden answering cry from off the face of the mere - a cry that had in it an indefinable touch of pathos. Into the midst of a little company of three wild duck resting on the water in fancied security, grim tragedy had entered unseen, and was claiming one of its number. Uttering shrill, pitiable cries, the bird strove frantically to rise from the lake, wildly beating the air with its wings in vain impotence to release itself from the invisible power that held it down as in a vice. From sedge and flag there issued forth a procession of other duck towards the place, marshalled by two stately swans, curiosity having mastered their fear of the 'humans' in the punt. They, too, were desirous to know the cause of the unusual commotion. Meanwhile, with wings and voice, the captive continued the unequal contest in an agony of futile effort; but the unseen was inexorable, and, while the other birds gathered wonderingly around, the unhappy duck was drawn slowly down beneath the surface, and the next instant, in vivid contrast to the despairing cry of life, there came a stillness as of death.

The mere had upheld its credit for big pike, and we, if we had not caught one, had at any rate been privileged to witness a spectacle that cannot often be vouchsafed to anglers' eyes.

Solving the Riddle of the Lady's Pike

Frederick Buller

In the first edition of *Mammoth Pike* I appealed for details of any big pike that would qualify for my 'Big Pike List' and/or more data or corrections to pike already listed. Among the many letters that I received was one written by a thirteen year old schoolboy which so impressed me that I recall it here.

Dear Mr Buller,

The business of [my letter] is a 36-pound pike which inhabits the window of Richardson's shop in East Bridge Street, Enniskillen. The pike, mounted inside a case, measures 45-50 inches; its maximum girth just behind the head could be 26 inches. I think that the pike in The Domesday Book of Mammoth Pike *that this fish most resembles is No. 179 on page 84 (the Dublin Museum Pike), although at the tail end of the Enniskillen pike where the body meets the tail, it is much slimmer and the fishes body tapers back more definitely than that on the fish in your book. The back of the fish is sound (no kinks) and the fins point backwards, so the fish is not a*

Williams-mounted pike. Unfortunately, there is no inscription on the case indicating by whom it was caught or where or when, although it is known to have been caught in Lough Erne.

The fish has a massively thick and deep shoulder, like the body of a bream. Its head is very similar to the pike I was previously discussing, in your book, having a beak-like mouth. Its fins look worn and are brownish and grey coloured. Its skin is a deepish brown-green colour, slightly faded through age. This fading of the skin-colour seems to be a characteristic of large Irish pike.

My overall impression of the fish is a very good fish not excellently mounted, but passably so. The grasses were obviously not meticulously chosen and look slightly awkward. However, you should not just take my word for all this but have a look at the fish personally. I promise you that this fish exists if you live in doubt.

I thought this could be of help to you if you were planning on another version of your Domesday Book. *I wish you luck if you undertake such an enterprise and hope you call to Enniskillen over the matter of the pike I am concerned with, although if you cannot fit such a trip into your schedule I should be pleased to photograph the fish for you. Good luck.*

Yours sincerely,
John D. McKeagney (age 13)

In my reply to Master John, besides thanking him for 'discovering' Richardson's Pike and for his report, I pointed out the difficulties of photographing cased pike. I then made a mental note that I would visit Mr Richardson's shop as soon as two or three calls in the general area demanded a visit. In January 1982, nearly two years later, I received the nicest letter that I have ever had from a bank manager:

Dear Mr Buller,
There is a large cased pike in Richardson's shop at Enniskillen. I have looked at it and John Richardson has measured it (from outside the glass case). It would appear to be about 46 inches long and about 11 inches deep. No doubt more accurate measurements could be taken, particularly if the case were opened.

Having compared it with the photographs in your books, it seems to me to be a particularly 'fat' fish.

If you write to John Richardson, c/o Richardson's Ltd, East Bridge Street, Enniskillen, Co. Fermanagh, Northern Ireland, he may provide you with more accurate measurements and details of its capture. It is reputed to have been caught in Lough Erne by a lady!

Do not imagine from this letter that I am an accomplished pike angler, far from it. I am an enthusiastic amateur, with aspirations to catch a big pike, that's all. Actually, I feel that living in this area (Enniskillen) puts me, geographically speaking only, in an excellent position for the pursuit of big pike.

If one were to believe all the stories that one hears of very big fish, thirty pounds would seem small. However, while I do not really believe most of what I hear about big pike, the stories fire my imagination and I think to myself 'maybe a few of them could be true'. I hope, in time, to prove at least one such story to have been well founded.

Yours sincerely,
Hugh Mannix, Enniskillen.

I noted Hugh Mannix's remark 'It is reputed to have been caught in Lough Erne by a lady'. And wondered if this pike could be the pike already listed in my book, i.e. pike No. 60, first reported in *The Daily Mail* on 25th March, 1926:

43lb Pike Caught

A huge pike has been caught on Lough Erne, Ireland, in a remarkable manner by Mrs McManus, of Inniskeen Island, a herd's [shepherd's] wife. Seeing the fish in the rushes in shallow water, she jabbed her two fingers into its eyes, blinding it, and then hauled it into her boat. The pike was 4 foot in length, 26 inches in girth and 43lb in weight. The fish is to be stuffed.

With the possibility that the pike first reported to me by the schoolboy, John McKeagney, (and judged in the absence of any legend on the case to be a 36lb pike) was in fact Mrs McManus's missing 43lb pike - I wrote to Mr Richardson in these terms.

Dear Mr Richardson,
I have been told by two of your local pike anglers that you have a large cased pike on your premises. Hugh Mannix of the Bank of Ireland tells me that he thinks it was caught by a lady!

I don't know whether you are familiar with my book The Domesday Book of Mammoth Pike *or not (Mr Mannix has a copy) but in it there is a story of a Mrs McManus's pike taken from Lough Erne in 1926. Could this be your pike? I would be very pleased to have any data on your fish and I would be pleased to pay to have it photographed by a professional photographer. I enclose a SAE for your reply.*

Here is Mr John Richardson's reply dated 2nd February, 1982:

Dear Mr Buller,
Thank you for your interesting letter. My information on the cased pike was received in my boyhood from an old employee who spent over sixty years with our firm. The card with the details at that time was visible and legible also. I believe that this is the pike attributed to Mrs McManus. You will be welcome to take a photo when next you are in Enniskillen.

Yours sincerely,
John Richardson

There is just one more twist to this story; on 19th February, 1981 I received another note from Hugh Mannix together with a photocopy of a report that appeared in the *Impartial Reporter* dated 11th February, 1982:

Large Pike

The origin of the large pike in John Richardson's shop has aroused some speculation. Is it or is it not the famous Inniskeen fish? This week Gerry McLarnan, from Drumcor Hill, Cornagrade, Enniskillen, called to tell me how the fish was caught. Gerry's father, Billy, is a nephew of the late Mrs Kathleen McManus who caught the pike. The story of its capture has been handed down through the family. Gerry recounted that Mrs McManus had been in Enniskillen and was returning home by boat to Inniskeen Island. The weather had been stormy and the land around the lake had flooded.

Mrs McManus saw something splashing in the shallow and when she went to investigate she discovered it was a huge pike. In those days many people living in Fermanagh supplemented their diet by fishing and so Mrs McManus ran to the house. Returning with a pitchfork she captured the pike. It may well have ended up on the dining table but Mr Morris, known locally as 'Morris the Jew' (he had an antique shop in East Bridge Street), who was a keen angler, was given the fish by

Mrs McManus and he had it stuffed. It was then put on display in Lemon's shop which was later to become Richardson's. Gerry recalls that the pike was caught around 1920 and that his father maintained it weighed about 48lb.

Well the mystery of the cased pike - with no inscription - is well and truly solved and the manner in which it was taken finally resolved - and it is a matter of some satisfaction to me because I never have believed that a woman would even attempt to haul, let alone attempt and then succeed in hauling a 43lb pike into her boat in the manner described by *The Daily Mail* some fifty-six years before.

In May 1982 I met Hugh Mannix at his bank in Enniskillen during which meeting Hugh agreed to have the pike in Richardson's shop photographed (my own attempt was thwarted by the town's half closing day) and Mrs McManus's island investigated.In due course (July 1982) I received a photograph of the pike with this note:

. . . For your information Inniskeen is a large island covering perhaps 1,000 acres situated to the left of the River Erne some two miles upstream of Enniskillen. The island contains the remains of an old monastic settlement surrounded by a graveyard and this brought to mind the words of Percy French's well known poem, 'The Four Farleys':

Are you that Francis Farley
I met so long ago,
In the bogs above Belmullet
In the County of Mayo.
The long legged freckled Francis
With deep set smiling eyes,
Which seemed to take their colour
From the ever changing skies.

That put his flute together
As I sketched the distant scene,
And played me 'Planxteen Kelly'
And the 'Graves of Innishkeen'.

Kind regards and apologies for the delay.

Yours sincerely,
Hugh Mannix

The Sergeant's Pike

'Benwyan', The Fishing Gazette *(23rd February, 1901)*

It was one of those bright days I told you of - flat calm - the sun beating down on the lake and back into your face till it shone like a red railway light, and the skin got as tight as a drumhead. The flies came up Jack-in-the-box fashion, straightway bolting into the blue, so there was not a fish to be got.

A little after lunch time our three boats, attracted like grugles floating in a teacup, came together. As they approached there was a commotion in one of them, to which a strongly curved rod and a cheer drew attention; then, after a bit, two of the occupants were engaged with the landing-net on the off side, over which something glittering came in. A few among us spectators betrayed excitement, while the stalwart ex-sergeant rested on his oar, winked, and audibly smiled, saying, "The old bottle trick!" He was right - a clear glass one made fast to the line, and dexterously landed, *pour encourager les autres.*

The sold ones were laughed at till the Englishman's cheeks split; the pipes were alight, while we lay with the boats almost touching, and told yarns piscatorial. Someone spoke of the £50 reward for a 50lb pike.

"Pity I did not hear of that in time, sir," quoth the sergeant. "Why? Are there any big 'uns here?"

"Faith and there are. Paddy's father there was attacked by one of them in a bog creek, and, only for the grape he had, would hardly have escaped being badly wounded, for he had taken his breeches off to keep them dry, and I picked up the skull of another, near two feet long, on that shore there below, when gathering flies."

"But did you never see one yourself, sergeant?"

"Yes, once. It was this way: I had to go over to the police barrack, at the far end of Armagh Bay, on business, so I threw a pike rod and baits into the boat, intending to troll along and kill two birds with one stone. Nothing happened till I was into the bay, then I got stuck in a big fish. There was a long fight; but it was no use, I could not get him near enough to see what size he was. I let him alone for a while to tire himself, towing the boat about. Time was passing, and I was apt to miss the head constable, so it was the best thing I could do to run ashore at that little white marly sort of a beach you see yonder, to try and land him - I was fairly strong, for often when an ass couldn't bring its load out of the bog I'd make them take him from the shafts, and pull it out by myself. Well, I leant on the oars and shot the boat far in on the land, then I jumped out, got the line over my shoulder, and walked up the slope, putting out all my strength; the line cut into the leather patch on my shooting coat, and the footmarks I left were deep enough to last a year. I heard the big splash in the water as I brought him a bit farther for safety, and when I turned to see - I can't tell you the size of him, but I give you my word, sir, the lough fell a foot, be the same more or less. He was an awful big fish; I had a job to get him into the boat, and another to get her off the shore, the water being so much farther out. I know it's a fact, for the head constable noticed it, and when the postman came round the lough next day he said they told him a lot of the old oak snags under water at Aghenah had come above the surface just when it happened. Of course, it wasn't a thing to brag of, but they were 'alligating' about it for a long time all round the lough, and, more by token, when I went to his Reverence to get my pension paper signed he had the story too, and he told me to repent."

Should this voracious narrative be thought 'nutty',

I disclaim responsibility for that. I only heard it once, then and there, from the sergeant himself, and if any one doubts its substantial accuracy I think I could find his address.

Our Englishman made a note of it, but others may not have heard it before.

The Freshwater Shark

From Canadian Wilds *(1907) by Martin Hunter*

Martin Hunter started work with the Hudson's Bay Company in 1863. After forty years in various posts he gained the experience that was to provide the background for his book *Canadian Wilds* (1907).

The following account in a chapter headed 'Voracious Pike' paints a delightful picture of the earlier Canadian rural scene - so far as pike threatened a valuable fishery.

Calling the pike the freshwater shark is a name well applied, for he is bold and anything that comes his way is food for his maw. It is a known fact to those who have studied its habits that he will eat frogs, young ducks, musquash, in fact, anything that happens to be in front of him, not even barring his own offspring. How destructive they are in a trout or whitefish lake is well known.

One of the lakes on which I was stationed years ago was said to have been, formerly, good for whitefish, but was now almost nude of this staple food of the dwellers at the post, brought about by the increasing number of pike.

As I was likely to be in charge, for a few years at least, I set to work to destroy these marauders. The lake is only a mile and a half long by a quarter broad. It discharges into a large river by a shallow creek, but, by this creek, no doubt, many pike were added to the number at each spawning time.

The creek took my attention first, and we staked it from side to side with pickets six feet high and planted them about two inches apart.

At the back or river side of this barrier we kept some old, almost useless, nets set continuously. They were doubled so that no small sized pike could pass. This was done during the low water in August.

My next move was to employ every boy, girl and old woman about the post trolling for pike. We supplied them with the trolls and lines and paid them a cent apiece for every pike over a foot long.

During this trolling process we kept some nets of large mesh, set purposely for the bigger ones. For days and weeks there must have been landed on an average a hundred a day, and yet they came. As most of the pay was taken out in cheap 'bullseyes' at a cent apiece, the real outlay in money was not considerable.

The following spring we inaugurated another system of warfare against the pests, and that was by paddling quietly around the bays and shooting them while they lay spawning and basking in the sun and shallow water.

Often three or four would be clustered together. A shot would not kill the whole, but it would stun them so we could finish them with the paddle.

One that was killed in this way measured 39 inches long and weighed 35lb. A fish of this size was good eating, and therefore used at the post.

The small, slimy ones, however, were burned in numbers on a brush heap.

With such persistent and continued onslaught on our part, at the end of the first year their numbers were very noticeably decreased, and at the close of the following summer they were positively scarce, and a very welcome number of whitefish stocked our lake in their place.

I resided at that post for twelve years, and we were never in want of the finest fish for the post's consumption.

Before closing this sketch I must tell one anecdote about a pike, even if I lay myself open to be disbelieved by the reader. I am well aware that fish stories stand in bad repute and the veracity of the narrator doubted. The following is positively true and came under my notice:

Years before the foregoing part of my story happened I was stationed on the height of land north of Lake Superior, and one afternoon portaged my canoe over into a small chain of beaver lakes hunting for signs.

It was a 'still, calm day', as some high-flown writer would put it. A feather dropped would have fallen straight to the earth. I was paddling very quietly out into the lake from the portage when I noticed something moving very gently on the surface a few yards ahead of the canoe. Getting closer I made this out to be the fin of some fish moving sluggishly. Pushing the canoe further in advance with noiseless knife strokes of the paddle, I got close enough to see it was a pike with a whitefish half protruding from its mouth and almost dead from suffocation.

This, I thought, is a rare occurrence for a person to witness, and gently reaching out my hand I inserted my thumb and finger into the eye sockets and lifted both into the canoe.

On getting ashore at the next portage I forced open the jaws of the pike, and the whitefish dropped from them. The half that had been inside the pike's mouth was quite decomposed, while the part out in the water was comparatively fresh.

In trying to swallow this fish, which was two-thirds the pike's own length, he had distended his jaws to the utmost, but they only opened enough to reach near the back fin, and here fixing his teeth in savage fury the biter had bitten more than he could eat. He was equally unable to disgorge himself as he was incapable of swallowing, and thus by his greediness he brought on his doom.

Noticing his stomach was in a distended shape caused me to rip it open with my knife, and out tumbled the remains of a smaller whitefish, almost quite digested, which had been swallowed whole and would have measured nearly a foot long.

It was gluttony and not hunger that caused him to reach an untimely end, a moral for greedy little boys.

Putting the Jeans on for a Big Pike

A stuffed pike, mounted by taxidermist Chris Elliott, attracted the attention of a young lady called Jackie when she attended a recent exhibition held in London. She told Chris the story of a big pike that she and her father caught on Lough Sheelin some eight years before. Chris passed the data on to me and my letter to her father resulted in my being sent a full account of their fine catch:

It was a blazing hot August day and the wedding guests were leaving the Sheelin Shamrock Hotel on the shores of Lough Sheelin in County Cavan.

At last some of the guests were leaving, that was, of course, until Jackie and I arrived on the scene carrying the two pike. There was a chorus of "Look at the size of those fish!" From the crowd of people leaving the wedding reception, and there was a general movement in our direction.

The hotel proprietress, seeing the people in front of

the hotel, came out to investigate the reason, and upon seeing the pike quickly sent her youngest son, Damien, to bring the wedding photographer, who, oddly enough, expressed no surprise at being requested to photograph the fish as well as the bride.

We had started our day by taking one of the boats from the hotel out on the lake, ostensibly to fish, but the day was hopeless for anything other than sunbathing. The sun blazed out of a cloudless sky and the lake was like a mirror.

We lazed around in the boat and motored quietly along to Church Island. Jackie was wearing a bathing suit and a straw hat. It was quite positively not a fishing day.

We rowed around Church Island to the deeper side opposite the reed beds and shipped the oars.

I rooted around in my tackle box looking for a suitable spinner and put on a black Koster spoon. It was a thick, heavy, black spoon, but I had no reason for using it other than that I had had it for years, and had never, ever used it before. I flipped it 50 yards from the boat towards the reed bed, and let it sink, which it did, very quickly. I began to turn the reel handle. The lure came to an abrupt halt when it had travelled about 10 yards.

"Bottom," I said.

The 'bottom' began to move! A pike about 3 feet long erupted from the lake! I was more surprised than the fish!

I passed the rod across to Jackie. "Play that lad for a while," I said, "it's going to take a brave while to bring him in!"

She played the fish for about ten minutes or so. It was a spectacular performance. It jumped repeatedly - more like a trout than a pike! The boat rocked in the flat calm.

Finally, she played it close enough to the boat for me to be able to reach over and gaff it in the jaw. It was a good, fit pike weighing 16lb.

"That performance will have scared every fish for miles around," I said.

"In any case that could be the fish of a life-time - we'll never get another one as big as that."

So saying, I flipped the spoon into the lake, within feet of the first cast.

It didn't get the chance to reach the bottom. There was a wrenching strike and I was into another fish! This one stayed down. A violent shaking vibrated through the top of the rod, followed by the scream of the line off the reel, as the fish made a 20 yard run. It stopped. I reeled in line. Off it went again.

I badly wanted Jackie to feel the power of this fish,

so whilst maintaining my grip on the butt, we crossed hands and I transferred the rod to her control.

Line screamed off the reel once more. Jackie frantically took up the slack, rod held high, shouting, "It's too big, Daddy, take it back!"

Amused, I called back, "Keep a firm hold on it, you'll be all right."

She checked the reel, the fish moved the boat, but even then I never imagined that this fish could possibly be bigger than the first one.

"He's coming up," she screamed, standing up in the boat, with the rod held high over her head and reeling like mad. He was coming up alright!! Five yards from the boat! There was an explosion of water as he made three consecutive jumps. We were drenched with spray, and a wave was set up which rocked the boat. It was twice as big as the first pike!

Jackie screamed, "Take the rod, take the rod, he's too big and don't get him into the boat until I get my jeans on!"

We transferred the rod again. I couldn't for the life of me think what her jeans had to do with getting the fish into the boat.

This pike was really going now. Throwing his full length into the air and crashing back into the lake, spray flying in all directions. Jackie was frantically struggling into her jeans, rocking the boat as much as the pike.

"Some performance this," I thought.

Finally she was dressed. "What about taking the rod now?" I asked.

"I'll have to gaff it - it's too big for you!"

The pike was so big that I was wondering how on earth I was ever going to get it into the boat! We transferred the rod for the third time and the pike took off on a long run into deep water. I have had brilliant sport with quite small pike on light tackle, but I had always found on previous occasions that big pike were something of a disappointment, and quite frequently came easily either to the bank or the boat. This lad was the exception that proved the rule.

It fought for at least another twenty minutes, and then came slowly to the surface, and after a few dashes away from the boat, which were impossible to stop, came within reach.

I was, by now, kneeling on the bottom boards, with a firm grip on the gaff with my right hand, and an even firmer one around the seat with my left. I wasn't too sure who would win this battle, but I was making sure as far as I could that I wouldn't be joining the pike in the lake.

At last, Jackie, handling the rod very well, considering

that she was scared witless, managed to bring the pike within the range of the gaff. I drove the gaff into the jaw and heaved back. The water exploded, but the fish slid over the gunwale and into the boat. It was a huge fish 50 inches long, a foot deep and it weighed just over 35lb. *

That is really all there is to tell, except that when we were motoring back down the lake, I asked Jackie why she was so concerned about putting her jeans on when the second pike was hooked.

She replied with typical female logic, which, of course, I do not understand, "I was afraid that it might bite me if I wasn't wearing my jeans."

* The pike which was over 35lb when caught, weighed 34¾lb when weighed twenty-four hours later by the Inland Fisheries Trust at Lough Sheelin. A scale analysis proved the fish to be twelve years old. It held the record for a pike caught in the Irish Republic during 1973 and won a gold medal award from ABU for its captors.

Pike on the Fly

Edward Fitzgibbon or 'Ephemera' as he was known to his readers, was probably the first writer to define what a pike fly is supposed to convey to a hungry pike. In *A Handbook of Angling*, 1847, he recommended that pike flies should be purchased from Mr Blacker of Dean Street, Soho, who tied them as imitations of a sand-martin or a swallow.

Readers who think that such a dressing is a bit far fetched should dwell on the following incident described in *The Fishing Gazette*, 1883, by Mr H. Band, who witnessed it near Leipzig in Germany. Mr Band was fishing in the Mulde, near Castle Zschepplin. He says:

A few paces below me I noticed three young sand-martins perched on a bough which over-hung the water. They could hardly fly, and the old ones were fluttering about them. My float lay motionless on the surface. Suddenly there was a tremendous splash in the water directly down under the withie bough, which swung up and down. One bird was still on the bough, and another, after fluttering about a little, again settled down on it. I looked on in amazement; the waves, caused by the splash, spread over the river, the surface became smooth and still again, but one bird was missing.

A bite at my line recalled my attention to fishing; but presently there was another splash under the bough, which swayed about again - the other bird was missing, and now only one remained, balancing itself with difficulty on the swinging branch. That the thief was a pike was quite evident. I stuck my rod-butt into the soft bank, and quietly approached the spot, soon finding a convenient place from which to reconnoitre. Steadily, I watched for a long time. The final dash of the pike occurred so violently, so suddenly - and this time from the side where I had been sitting - that I could only get an instant's view of what had happened. The third sand-martin was gone. The swaying bough grew still again, and all was over.

Another Great Pike from Whittlesea

The Great Pike of Whittlesea Mere was captured when the mere (the largest lake in southern England) was drained in 1851, although J. Wentworth Day in *The Angler's Pocket Book* says it was drained in 1849. The pike weighed 52lb and measured 55 inches long.

Despite the disappearance of the mere, the magic of the name as regards huge pike, lived on as the next photograph witnesses. In the 1990s a friendly dealer in cased fish brought another Whittlesea Mere pike to me. This one weighed 42½lb and was 45 inches long. The legend reads:

The last of the Great Giants of Whittlesea Mere - caught in a drag-net in Bevills Leam at the north-west point of the mere, March 1875, by John Crampton. Supposed to have escaped when the drainage took place. Ducks being lost this old pike was observed to pull them under. He tasted like pork.

Well, if it did escape from Whittlesea, it lived another twenty-four years before it was killed, or another twenty-six years if you believe Wentworth Day.

Myths and Legends

The pike is an important mythical fish in Germany and this story, sent by Henning Stilke, who, himself is writing a book (in German) about pike stories from that part of the world, is an example of the place they hold in the angler's imagination.

The Sunken Castle

Legend has it that deep beneath the waters of the lake of Stintenburg, in north-east Germany, there lies an old castle. The place is now commonly called *Borgstedenort* - 'place of the castle'. People say the submerged castle is cursed, and fishermen often observe, around midnight, a strange gleam of light coming up from the depths of the lake. This, they say, is the light from the many windows of the sunken castle.

Within the lake, so the legend goes, lives an ancient pike, his head grown over with moss, and in his mouth a key. The key is the key to the castle, and if any fisherman with the name Bulow catches the pike and takes the key, then the castle will rise out of the depths, the fisherman will be able to open the doors and enter all the rooms. Everything that he finds therein will become his.

(Bulow is not an uncommon name in north-west Germany, but it is the name of a big noble family, and perhaps the story implies that the fish can only be caught by a noble man. We can only guess!)

The Creation of the Pike

Myths and legends abound about the pike, and this folk-tale from the Syrjanen - a tribe of eastern Finland - show just how deeply they have been embedded in some cultures.

The story goes that the Devil created the pike. And he went to God and said, "Today I created the pike."

God responds, "I have also created the pike."

"But how will we tell them apart, yours and mine?" says the Devil.

"That's easy," said God, "Mine have a sign. A cross in their head." [ie, a cruciform bone].

"Mine don't have a cross," said the Devil.

"Let's go to the riverbank and see," responded God.

So, they went to the bank of the river and looked into the water.

The Devil said to God, "You call your pikes, first."

God called his pikes. The pikes came to him.

Then the Devil called his pikes, but not one came to him. "I have lost my pikes," he said. Then he examines all of God's pikes, and sure enough they all have a cross in the head. "Those don't belong to me," he said.

Then they went home.

With thanks to Henning Stilke, who found the story re-told in Volksdichtung der Komi (Syrjanen) *by D.R. Fokos-Fuchs, Budapest, 1951.*